# Selection of French Riviera Hotels and Restaurants

Where do you start? Choosing a hotel or restaurant in a place you're not familiar with can be daunting. To help you find your way amid the bewildering variety, we have made a selection from the *Red Guide to France 1990* published by Michelin, the recognized authority on gastronomy and accommodation throughout Europe.

Our own Berlitz criteria have been price and location. In the hotel section, for a double room with bath but without breakfast, Higher-priced means above 900 F, Medium-priced 500–900 F, Lower-priced below 500 F. As to restaurants, for a meal consisting of a starter, a main course and a dessert, Higher-priced means above 250 F, Medium-priced 150–250 F. Lower-priced below 150 F. $$$ stands for Higher-priced, $$ for Medium-priced and $ for Lower-priced. Special features where applicable are also given. Most hotels and restaurants close down a fortnight or a month per year and many restaurants have a regular weekly closing day (or days). Both a check to make certain that they are open and advance reservations are advisible. Prices for French Riviera hotels and restaurants generally include a service charge.

For a wider choice of hotels and restaurants, we strongly recommend you obtain the authoritative Michelin *Red Guide to France,* which gives a comprehensive and reliable picture of the situation throughout the country.

## ANTIBES

### Hotels

**Bleu Marine $**
rue des 4 Chemins
06600 Antibes
Tel. 93 74 84 84
*18 rooms. View. No restaurant.*

**du Cap d'Antibes $$$**
bd Kennedy
06600 Antibes
Tel. 93 61 39 01; tlx. 470763
*121 rooms. Pleasant, luxury hotel with large flowered garden giving onto the sea. Outdoor pool. Private beach. Tennis court.*

**La Gardiole $$**
chemin La Garoupe
06600 Antibes
Tel. 93 61 35 03
*21 rooms. Quiet situation. Garden. Outdoor dining.*

**Josse $$**
8 bd James Wyllie
06600 Antibes
Tel. 93 61 47 24
*22 rooms. View. No restaurant.*

**Mas Djoliba $**
29 av. Provence
06600 Antibes
Tel. 93 34 02 48; tlx. 461686
*14 rooms. Quiet position. Pleasant garden. Outdoor swimming pool.*

**Royal $$**
bd Mar.-Leclerc
06600 Antibes
Tel. 93 34 03 09
*38 rooms. View. Beach with bathing facilities. Outdoor dining.*

### Restaurants

**Bacon $$$**
bd Bacon
06600 Antibes
Tel. 93 61 50 02
*Notably good cuisine. View of the Baie des Anges. Outdoor dining.*

**Du Bastion $**
1 av. Gén.-Maizière
06600 Antibes
Tel. 93 34 13 88
*Outdoor dining.*

**L'Écurie Royale $$**
33 rue Vauban
06600 Antibes
Tel. 93 34 76 20

**La Marguerite $$**
11 rue Sadi Carnot
06600 Antibes
Tel. 93 34 08 27

**Les Vieux Murs $$**
av. Amiral de Grasse
06600 Antibes
Tel. 93 34 06 73
*Outdoor dining.*

## BEAULIEU-SUR-MER

### Hotels

**Carlton Résidence $$**
9 bis av. Albert-1er
06310 Beaulieu-sur-Mer
Tel. 93 01 06 02
*29 rooms. Garden. No restaurant.*

### Métropole $$$
bd Mar.-Leclerc
06310 Beaulieu-sur-Mer
Tel. 93 01 00 08; tlx. 470304
*50 rooms. Quiet situation. Large
terrace overlooking the sea.
Garden. Outdoor swimming pool.
Beach with bathing facilities.
Notably good cuisine.*

### La Réserve $$$
bd Mar.-Leclerc
06310 Beaulieu-sur-Mer
Tel. 93 01 00 01; tlx. 470301
*50 rooms. Quiet situation. Pleas-
ant, luxuriously appointed hotel
on seafront. View. Outdoor swimming pool. Outdoor dining.*

## BIOT

### Restaurants

### Les Terraillers $$
06410 Biot
Tel. 93 65 01 59
*Situated in a 16th-century former
pottery. Outdoor dining. Notably
good cuisine.*

## BORMES-LES-MIMOSAS

### Hotels

### Paradis Hotel $
Mont des Roses
83230 Bormes-les-Mimosas
Tel. 94 71 06 85
*20 rooms. Quiet hotel. View. Gar-
den. Outdoor dining.*

### Le Mirage $$
rte Stade
83230 Bormes-les-Mimosas
Tel. 94 71 09 83; tlx. 404603
*37 rooms. Quiet hotel. View of
the bay and islands. Outdoor
swimming pool. Garden. Hotel
tennis court.*

### Restaurants

### La Cassole $$
ruelle Moulin
83230 Bormes-les-Mimosas
Tel. 94 71 14 86

### Tonnelle des Délices $$
place Gambetta
83230 Bormes-les-Mimosas
Tel. 94 71 34 84

## CAGNES-SUR-MER

### Hotels

### Le Cagnard $$
rue Pontis-Long (Haut-de-
Cagnes)
06800 Cagnes-sur-Mer
Tel. 93 20 73 21; tlx. 462223
*13 rooms. Pleasant hotel in quiet
situation. View. Notably good
cuisine. Outdoor dining.*

### Les Collettes $
38 chemin des Collettes
06800 Cagnes-sur-Mer
Tel. 93 20 80 66
*13 rooms. Quiet position. View.
Swimming pool. No restaurant.*

**Tiercé Hotel $**
33 bd Kennedy
06800 Cagnes-sur-Mer
Tel. 93 20 02 09
*23 rooms. View. No restaurant.*

## Restaurants

**Peintres $**
7l montée Bourgade (Haut de Cagnes)
06800 Cagnes-sur-Mer
Tel. 93 20 83 08
*View.*

**Villa du Cros $$**
Port du Cros
06800 Cagnes-sur-Mer
Tel. 93 07 57 83
*Outdoor dining.*

## CANNES

## Hotels

**Beau Séjour $$**
5 rue Fauvettes
06400 Cannes
Tel. 93 39 63 00; tlx. 470975
*46 rooms. Outdoor swimming pool. Garden.*

**Carlton Intercontinental $$$**
58 bd Croisette
06400 Cannes
Tel. 93 68 91 68; tlx. 470720
*325 rooms. Pleasant, luxury hotel. View. Beach with bathing facilities. La Côte restaurant.*

**Corona $**
55 rue d'Antibes
06400 Cannes
Tel. 93 39 69 85
*20 rooms. No restaurant.*

**Embassy $$**
6 rue Bône
06400 Cannes
Tel. 93 38 79 02; tlx. 470081
*60 rooms.*

**La Madone $$**
5 av. Justinia
06400 Cannes
Tel. 93 43 57 87
*22 rooms. Cosy establishment. Quiet situation. Garden. No restaurant.*

**Majestic $$$**
bd Croisette
06400 Cannes
Tel. 93 68 91 00; tlx. 470787
*249 rooms. Pleasant, luxury hotel. View. Outdoor swimming pool. Beach with bathing facilities. Garden. Outdoor dining.*

**Martinez $$$**
73 bd Croisette
06400 Cannes
Tel. 93 94 30 30; tlx. 470708
*421 rooms. Luxury hotel. View Outdoor swimming pool. Beach with bathing facilities. Garden. Outdoor dining. La Palme d'Or restaurant. L'Orangeraie restaurant.*

**Molière $**
5 rue Molière
06400 Cannes
Tel. 93 38 16 16
*34 rooms. Garden. No restaurant.*

**Paris $$**
34 bd d'Alsace
06400 Cannes
Tel. 93 38 30 89; tlx. 470995
*48 rooms. Outdoor swimming
pool. Garden. No restaurant.*

**Select $**
16 rue H. Vagliano
06400 Cannes
Tel. 93 99 51 00
*30 rooms.*

## Restaurants

**Caveau 30 $**
45 rue Félix-Faure
06400 Cannes
Tel. 93 39 06 33
*Outdoor dining.*

**La Croisette $**
15 rue Cdt-André
06400 Cannes
Tel. 93 39 86 06

**Le Festival $$**
52 bd Croisette
06400 Cannes
Tel. 93 38 04 81
*Outdoor dining.*

**Le Monaco $**
15 rue 24-août
06400 Cannes
Tel. 93 38 37 76

**L'Olivier $**
9 rue Rouguière
06400 Cannes
Tel. 93 39 91 63

**La Palme d'Or $$$**
73 bd Croisette
06400 Cannes
Tel. 92 98 30 18; tlx. 470708
*Notably good cuisine.*

**Royal Gray $$$**
2 rue des Etats-Unis
06400 Cannes
Tel. 93 99 04 59; tlx. 470744
*Excellent cuisine. Outdoor dining.
Elegant contemporary decor.*

## CAVALIÈRE

## Hotels

**Le Club $$$**
83980 Le Lavandou
Tel. 94 05 80 14; tlx. 420317
*26 rooms. Pleasant, elegant hotel
beside the sea. View. Tennis court.
Outdoor swimming pool. Beach
with bathing facilities.
Garden. Outdoor dining.*

## ÈZE

## Hotels

**Hermitage du Col d'Èze $**
06360 Eze-Village
Tel. 93 41 00 68
*14 rooms. View. Outdoor dining.*

### Restaurants

**Château de la Chèvre d'Or $$$**
rue Barri
06360 Èze-Village
Tel. 93 41 12 12
*Pleasant restaurant with notably good cuisine. Overlooking the sea. Outdoor swimming pool.*

**Le Grill du Château $$**
06360 Èze-Village
Tel. 93 41 00 17
*Outdoor dining.*

## FAYENCE

### Hotels

**Moulin de la Camandoule $**
83440 Fayence
Tel. 94 76 00 84
*11 rooms. Pleasant hotel in a former oil mill. Garden. Outdoor swimming pool. Outdoor dining.*

### Restaurants

**France $**
place République
83440 Fayence
Tel. 94 76 00 14
*Outdoor dining. Reservation essential.*

## GRASSE

### Hotels

**Panorama $**
2 place Cours
06130 Grasse
Tel. 93 36 80 80; tlx. 970908
*36 rooms. No restaurant.*

## GRIMAUD

### Hotels

**La Boulangerie $$**
83310 Grimaud
Tel. 94 43 23 16
*10 rooms. Quiet hotel. View. Garden. Outdoor swimming pool. Hotel tennis court. Outdoor dining.*

**Coteau Fleuri $**
83310 Grimaud
Tel. 94 43 20 17
*14 rooms. Quiet hotel. View. Garden. Outdoor dining.*

### Restaurants

**Café de France $**
83310 Grimaud
Tel. 94 43 20 05
*Outdoor dining.*

## JUAN-LES-PINS

### Hotels

**Alexandra $**
rue Pauline
06160 Juan-les-Pins
Tel. 93 61 01 36
*20 rooms. Beach with bathing facilities.*

**Juana $$$**
la Pinède av. G.-Gallice
06160 Juan-les-Pins
Tel. 93 61 08 70; tlx. 470778
*45 rooms. Pleasant hotel in quiet situation. Outdoor swimming pool. Private beach. Outdoor dining. La Terrasse restaurant.*

**Juan Beach $**
5 rue Oratoire
06160 Juan-les-Pins
Tel. 93 61 02 89
*28 rooms. Quiet situation. Beach
with bathing facilities. Garden.
Outdoor dining.*

**Mimosas $$**
rue Pauline
06160 Juan-les-Pins
Tel. 93 61 04 16
*37 rooms. Quiet hotel in a park.
Swimming pool. No restaurant.*

## Restaurants

**Le Perroquet $**
av. G.-Gallice
06160 Juan-les-Pins
Tel. 93 61 02 20
*Outdoor dining.*

## MENTON

## Hotels

**Aiglon $$**
7 av. Madone
06500 Menton
Tel. 93 57 55 55
*35 rooms. Outdoor swimming
pool. Garden. No restaurant.*

**Méditerranée $**
5 rue République
06500 Menton
Tel. 93 28 25 25; tlx. 461361
*90 rooms.*

**Pin Doré $**
16 av. F.-Faure
06500 Menton
Tel. 93 28 31 00
*42 rooms. View. Outdoor
swimming pool. Garden.
No restaurant.*

**Princess et Richmond $**
617 prom. Soleil
06500 Menton
Tel. 93 35 80 20
*43 rooms. View. No restaurant.*

**Viking $**
2 av. Gén.-de-Gaulle
06500 Menton
Tel. 93 57 95 85; tlx. 970331
*34 rooms. Outdoor swimming
pool.*

## Restaurants

**Chez Mireille-l'Ermitage $$**
1080 prom. Soleil
06500 Menton
Tel. 93 35 77 23
*View. Outdoor dining.*

**Paris-Palace $**
2 av. F.-Faure
06500 Menton
Tel. 93 35 86 66
*View. Outdoor dining.*

**Au Pistou $**
2 rue Fossan
06500 Menton
Tel. 93 57 45 89
*Outdoor dining.*

## MIRAMAR

### Hotels

**St-Christophe $$**
06590 Théoule
Tel. 93 75 41 36; tlx. 470878
*40 rooms. Pleasant hotel. View.
Beautiful garden. Outdoor swim-
ming pool. Private beach.*

**Tour de l'Esquillon $$**
06590 Théoule
Tel. 93 75 41 51
*25 rooms. Pleasant hotel. Access
to beach with bathing facilities
by private cable car. Beautiful
garden. Stunning view over sea.*

## MONACO

### Hotels

**Balmoral $$**
12 av. Costa
98000 Monaco
Tel. 93 50 62 37; tlx. 479436
*75 rooms. Quiet situation. View.
No restaurant.*

**Hermitage $$$**
square Beaumarchais
98000 Monaco
Tel. 93 50 67 31; tlx. 479432
*230 rooms. Pleasant hotel. View.
Indoor swimming pool. Baroque-
style dining room. Outdoor dining.*

**Paris $$$**
place Casino
98000 Monaco
Tel. 93 50 80 80: tlx. 469925
*206 rooms. Pleasant, luxury hotel.
View. Indoor swimming pool.
Garden. Louis XV restaurant.
Grill. Outdoor dining.*

### Restaurants

**Polpetta $**
6 av. Roqueville
98000 Monaco
Tel. 93 50 67 84
*Outdoor dining.*

**Roger Vergé Café $$**
Galerie du Sporting d'hiver
98000 Monaco
Tel. 93 25 86 12

## MOUGINS

### Hotels

**Arc Hotel $**
1082 rte Valbonne
06250 Mougins
Tel. 93 75 77 33; tlx. 462190
*44 rooms. Outdoor swimming
pool. Hotel tennis court. Outdoor
dining.*

**Mas Candille $$**
06250 Mougins
Tel. 93 90 00 85; tlx. 462131
*22 rooms. Quiet situation. View.
Terraced garden. Outdoor swim-
ming pool. Outdoor dining.*

### Restaurants

**Le Bistrot $**
06250 Mougins
Tel. 93 75 78 34

**Ferme de Mougins $$$**
St-Basile
06250 Mougins
Tel. 93 90 03 74; tlx. 970643
*Pleasant restaurant. Notably good
cuisine. Outdoor dining. Garden.*

**Feu Follet $**
place Mairie
06250 Mougins
Tel. 93 90 15 78
*Outdoor dining.*

**Moulin de Mougins $$$**
Notre-Dame-de-Vie
06250 Mougins
Tel. 93 75 78 24; tlx. 970732
*Superb cuisine. Pleasant
restaurant. Outdoor dining.*

**Relais à Mougins $$$**
06250 Mougins
Tel. 93 90 03 47; tlx. 462559
*Notably good cuisine. Outdoor
dining. Reservation essential.*

## LA NAPOULE

## Hotels

**La Calanque $**
av. H.-Clews
06210 Mandelieu-La Napoule
Tel. 93 49 95 11
*18 rooms. View. Outdoor dining.*

**Ermitage du Riou $$$**
06210 Mandelieu-La Napoule
Tel. 93 49 95 56; tlx. 470072

*42 rooms. Pleasant hotel. View.
Outdoor swimming pool. Garden.
Outdoor dining. Lamparo restau-
rant.*

## Restaurants

**Brocherie II $$**
06210 Mandelieu-La Napoule
Tel. 93 49 80 73
*View. Outdoor dining.*

## NICE

## Hotels

**Durante $**
16 av. Durante
06000 Nice
Tel. 93 88 84 40
*26 rooms. Quiet hotel. Garden.
No restaurant.*

**Georges $**
3 rue. H.-Cordier
06000 Nice
Tel. 93 86 23 41
*18 rooms. Quiet situation.
No restaurant.*

**Grand Hotel Aston $$**
12 av. F.-Faure
06000 Nice
Tel. 93 80 62 52; tlx. 470290
*160 rooms. Terrace on roof.*

**Harvey $**
18 av. de Suède
06000 Nice
Tel. 93 88 73 73; tlx. 461687
*62 rooms. No restaurant.*

**Marbella $**
120 bd Carnot
06000 Nice
Tel. 93 89 39 35
*14 rooms. View.*

**Méridien $$$**
1 prom. des Anglais
06000 Nice
Tel. 93 82 25 25; tlx. 470361
*305 rooms. View of the bay.
Outdoor swimming pool on the
roof. Outdoor dining.*

**Négresco $$$**
37 prom. des Anglais
06000 Nice
Tel. 93 88 39 51; tlx. 460040
*130 rooms. Pleasant, luxury hotel.
View. 16th- and 18th-century,
Empire, Napoleon III period
rooms and public rooms. La
Rotonde restaurant. Chantecler
restaurant.*

**La Pérouse $$$**
11 quai Rauba-Capeu
06000 Nice
Tel. 93 62 34 63; tlx. 461411
*63 rooms. Quiet hotel. View of
Nice and the Promenade des
Anglais. Outdoor swimming pool.*

**Plaza $$$**
12 av. Verdun
06000 Nice
Tel. 93 87 80 41; tlx. 460979
*187 rooms. View. Terrace on roof.*

**Sofitel Splendid $$**
50 bd Victor-Hugo
06000 Nice
Tel. 93 88 69 54; tlx. 460938
*116 rooms. View over the town.
Outdoor swimming pool on 8th
floor. Outdoor dining.*

**Victoria $$**
33 bd V.-Hugo
06000 Nice
Tel. 93 88 39 60; tlx. 461337
*39 rooms. Garden. No restaurant.*

## Restaurants

**Ane Rouge $$$**
7 quai Deux-Emmanuel
06300 Nice
Tel. 93 89 49 63

**Bon Coin Breton $**
5 rue Blacas
06000 Nice
Tel. 93 85 17 01

**Chantecler $$$**
37 prom. des Anglais
06000 Nice
Tel. 93 88 39 51; tlx. 460040
*Notably good cuisine.*

**Les Dents de la Mer $$**
2 rue St-François-de-Paule
06300 Nice
Tel. 93 80 99 16
*Seafood specialities. Original
decor. Outdoor dining.*

**Florian $$**
22 rue A.-Karr
06000 Nice
Tel. 93 88 86 60
*Notably good cuisine.*

**Aux Gourmets $$**
12 rue Dante
06000 Nice
Tel. 93 96 83 53

**La Merenda $**
4 rue Terrasse
06300 Nice
*Niçoise cuisine.*

**Rivoli $**
9 rue Rivoli
06000 Nice
Tel. 93 88 12 62

# PORT GRIMAUD

## Hotels

**Giraglia $$$**
83310 Cogolin
Tel. 94 56 31 33; tlx. 470494
*48 rooms. Quiet hotel. View of
the bay. Outdoor swimming pool.
Beach with bathing facilities.
Outdoor dining.*

## Restaurants

**La Tartane $$**
83310 Cogolin
Tel. 94 56 38 32
*Outdoor dining. View.*

# RAMATUELLE

## Hotels

**Le Baou $$$**
83350 Ramatuelle
Tel. 94 79 20 48; tlx. 462152

*41 rooms. Pleasant hotel in quiet
situation. Exceptional sea view.
Outdoor swimming pool. Outdoor
dining.*

# ROQUEBRUNE-CAP-MARTIN

## Hotels

**Vista Palace $$$**
Grande Corniche
06190 Roquebrune-Cap-Martin
Tel. 93 35 01 50; tlx. 461021
*62 rooms. Pleasant hotel. View
over Monaco. Outdoor swimming
pool. Garden.*

**Westminster $**
14 av. L.-Laurens
06190 Roquebrune-Cap-Martin
Tel. 93 35 00 68
*31 rooms. View. Garden.*

## Restaurants

**Au Grand Inquisiteur $**
rue Château
06190 Roquebrune-Cap-Martin
Tel. 93 35 05 37
*Country-style interior. Reservation
essential.*

**Hippocampe $$**
av. W.-Churchill
06190 Roquebrune-Cap-Martin
Tel. 93 35 81 91
*View of the bay and coast.
Outdoor dining.*

**Roquebrune $$$**
100 av. J.-Jaurès
06190 Roquebrune-Cap-Martin
Tel. 93 35 00 16
*View. Outdoor dining.*
*Reservation essential.*

## ST-JEAN-CAP-FERRAT

### Hotels

**Brise Marine $$**
av. J.-Mermoz
06230 St-Jean-Cap-Ferrat
Tel. 93 76 04 36
*15 rooms. Quiet situation. View of*
*the headland and bay. Garden.*
*Outdoor dining.*

**Grand Hotel du Cap-Ferrat $$$**
bd Gén.-de-Gaulle
06230 St-Jean-Cap-Ferrat
Tel. 93 76 00 21; tlx. 470184
*60 rooms. Pleasant, luxury hotel*
*in quiet situation. View. Large*
*park. Hotel tennis court. Outdoor*
*swimming pool beside the sea.*
*Beach with bathing facilities.*
*Private cable car. Notably good*
*cuisine. Outdoor dining.*

**Voile d'Or $$$**
06230 St-Jean-Cap-Ferrat
Tel. 93 01 13 13; tlx. 470317
*50 rooms. Pleasant hotel in quiet*
*situation. View of the port and*
*bay. Outdoor swimming pool.*
*Notably good cuisine. Outdoor*
*dining.*

### Restaurants

**Capitaine Cook $**
av. J. Mermoz
06230 St-Jean-Cap-Ferrat
Tel. 93 76 02 66
*Outdoor dining.*

**Le Sloop $$**
06230 St-Jean-Cap-Ferrat
Tel. 93 01 48 63
*Outdoor dining.*

## ST-PAUL

### Hotels

**Climat de France $**
06570 St-Paul
Tel. 93 32 94 24; tlx. 470167
*19 rooms. View. Outdoor swim-*
*ming pool. Outdoor dining.*

**La Colombe d'Or $$$**
06570 St-Paul
Tel. 93 32 80 02; tlx. 970607
*16 rooms. Pleasant hotel. Old-*
*Provence style. Modern paintings.*
*Outdoor swimming pool and*
*Roman garden. Outdoor dining.*

**Le Hameau $**
06570 St-Paul
Tel. 93 32 80 24
*14 rooms. Pleasant hotel. View.*
*Terraced garden. No restaurant.*

**Mas d'Artigny $$$**
06570 St-Paul
Tel. 93 32 84 54; tlx. 470601
*53 rooms. Luxury establishment*
*in quiet situation. View. Outdoor*
*swimming pool. Hotel tennis*
*court. Park. Notably good cuisine.*

**Orangers $$**
06570 St-Paul
Tel. 93 32 80 95
*9 rooms. Pleasant hotel in quiet situation. View. Beautiful garden. No restaurant.*

## ST-RAPHAËL

### Hotels

**Golf Hotel de Valescure $$**
close to Valescure golf course
83700 St-Raphaël
Tel. 94 82 40 31; tlx. 461085
*40 rooms. Pleasant hotel in quiet situation. View. Park. Outdoor swimming pool. Hotel tennis courts. Outdoor dining.*

**San Pedro $$**
close to Valescure golf course
av. Colonel Brooke
83700 St-Raphaël
Tel. 94 83 65 69
*28 rooms. Pleasant hotel in quiet situation. Park. Outdoor swimming pool.*

### Restaurants

**Pastorel $$**
54 rue Liberté
83700 St-Raphaël
Tel. 94 95 02 36
*Outdoor dining.*

**Sirocco $**
35 quai Albert 1er
83700 St-Raphaël
Tel. 94 95 39 99
*View.*

**La Voile d'Or $$**
1 bd Gén.-de-Gaulle
83700 St-Raphaël
Tel. 94 95 17 04
*View.*

## ST-TROPEZ

### Hotels

**Byblos $$$**
av. P.-Signac
83990 St-Tropez
Tel. 94 97 00 04; tlx. 470235
*70 rooms. Quiet situation. Richly furnished Provençal-style establishment. View. Outdoor swimming pool. Garden. Outdoor dining. La Braiserie restaurant.*

**Deï Marres $$**
83350 Ramatuelle
Tel. 94 97 26 68
*13 rooms. Quiet situation. View. Outdoor swimming pool. Garden. Hotel tennis court. No restaurant.*

**Lou Cagnard $**
av. P.-Roussel
83990 St-Tropez
Tel. 94 97 04 24
*19 rooms. Quiet situation. Garden. No restaurant.*

**Lou Troupelen $**
chemin des Vendanges
83990 St-Tropez
Tel. 94 97 44 88
*44 rooms. Quiet situation. Garden. No restaurant.*

### Mas de Chastelas $$$
83990 St-Tropez
Tel. 94 56 09 11; tlx. 462393
*21 rooms. Pleasant hotel in quiet situation. View. Park. Old silk-worm workshop among the vineyards. Outdoor swimming pool. Hotel tennis court. Outdoor dining.*

### Résidence de la Pinède $$$
83990 St-Tropez
Tel. 94 97 04 21; tlx. 470489
*34 rooms. Pleasant hotel in quiet situation. View. Outdoor swimming pool. Beach with bathing facilities. Outdoor dining.*

### La Tartane $$
rte des Salins
83990 St-Tropez
Tel. 94 97 21 23
*12 rooms. Quiet situation. View. Pleasant garden. Outdoor swimming pool. Outdoor dining.*

## Restaurants

### Le Chabichou $$$
av. Foch
83990 St-Tropez
Tel. 94 54 80 00; tlx. 461051
*Pleasant restaurant with notably good cuisine.*

### L'Échalotte $$
35 rue Allard
83990 St-Tropez
Tel. 94 54 83 26
*Outdoor dining.*

### Le Girelier $
83990 St-Tropez
Tel. 94 97 03 87
*View. Outdoor dining.*

### Leï Mouscardïn $$$
83990 St-Tropez
Tel. 94 97 01 53
*View of the bay.*

## STE-MAXIME

## Hotels

### Belle Aurore $$$
La Croisette
83120 Ste-Maxime
Tel. 94 96 02 45
*17 rooms. On seafront. View. Beach with bathing facilities. Outdoor swimming pool.*

### Calidianus $
83120 Ste-Maxime
Tel. 94 96 23 21
*33 rooms. Pleasant hotel in quiet situation. View. Outdoor swimming pool. Garden. Hotel tennis court. No restaurant.*

### «Croisette» Résidence $
bd Romarins
83120 Ste-Maxime
Tel. 94 96 17 75
*20 rooms. Quiet situation. Garden. No restaurant.*

### Poste $$
7 bd F.-Mistral
83120 Ste-Maxime
Tel. 94 96 18 33
*24 rooms. Outdoor swimming pool. Outdoor dining.*

### Le Revest $
av. J.-Jaurès
83120 Ste-Maxime
Tel. 94 96 19 60
*26 rooms. Outdoor swimming pool.*

### Restaurants

**L'Esquinade $$**
83120 Ste-Maxime
Tel. 94 96 01 65
*Outdoor dining. Seafood specialities.*

**La Gruppi $$**
av. Ch.-de-Gaulle
83120 Ste-Maxime
Tel. 94 96 03 61
*View. Outdoor dining. Seafood specialities.*

**Sans Souci $**
rue Paul-Bert
83120 Ste-Maxime
Tel. 94 96 18 26
*Outdoor dining.*

## VENCE

### Hotels

**Château du Domaine
St-Martin $$$**
06140 Vence
Tel. 93 58 02 02; tlx. 470282
*15 rooms. Pleasant, luxury hotel in quiet situation. View of Vence and coastline. Park. Outdoor swimming pool. Hotel tennis court. Notably good cuisine. Outdoor dining.*

**Floréal $$**
440 av. Rhin et Danube
06140 Vence
Tel. 93 58 64 40; tlx. 461613

*43 rooms. Outdoor swimming pool. Garden. No restaurant.*

**Miramar $**
plateau St-Michel
06140 Vence
Tel. 93 58 01 32
*17 rooms. Quiet situation. View. Garden. No restaurant.*

## VILLEFRANCHE

### Hotels

**Vauban $**
11 av. Gén.-de-Gaulle
06230 Villefranche
Tel. 93 01 71 20
*12 rooms. Louis XV decor. Pleasant garden. No restaurant.*

**Versailles $$**
av. Princesse-Grace
06230 Villefranche
Tel. 93 01 89 56; tlx. 970433
*46 rooms. View of the roadstead. Outdoor swimming pool. Outdoor dining.*

### Restaurants

**Mère Germaine $$**
quai Courbet
06230 Villefranche
Tel. 93 01 71 39
*View. Outdoor dining.*

# BERLITZ®

# FRENCH RIVIERA

By the staff of Berlitz Guides

# How to use our guide

- All the practical information, hints and tips that you will need before and during the trip start on page 100.

- For general background, see the sections The Region and its People, p.6, and A Brief History, p. 11.

- All the sights to see are listed between pages 20 and 77. Our own choice of sights most highly recommended is pinpointed by the Berlitz traveller symbol.

- Entertainment, nightlife and all other leisure activities are described between pages 77 and 90, while information on restaurants and cuisine is to be found on pages 91 to 99.

---

*Although we make every effort to ensure the accuracy of all the information in this book, changes occur incessantly. We cannot therefore take responsibility for facts, prices, addresses and circumstances in general that are constantly subject to alteration. Our guides are updated on a regular basis as we reprint, and we are always grateful to readers who let us know of any errors, changes or serious omissions they come across.*

---

Text: Suzanne Patterson
Photography: Monique Jacot
Layout: Doris Haldemann

We wish to thank Mr. and Mrs. Jean Fischbacher and Bob Davis, as well as the Société des Bains de Mer in Monte Carlo and the Caves de la Madeleine, Paris, for their help in the preparation of this guide. We're especially grateful to the tourist offices of Nice, Cannes and the Alpes Maritimes for their valuable assistance.

4 Cartography: Falk-Verlag, Hamburg.

# Contents

# The Region and its People

The Côte d'Azur, the Riviera, Provence, the Midi—call it what you will—this is the world's dream spot. Storied, chronicled, painted, photographed, it probably has more aura and more money than any other seacoast. It could also be called the French Gold Coast, with soaring real estate prices and cost-of-living among the world's highest.

*Port-Grimaud, the coast's newest little Venice, is built on canals.*

The Riviera calls up a picture of lolling millionaires, limpid sea and pink palaces of the F. Scott Fitzgerald era. From the fabled princes or rakes gambling at Monte Carlo to lissom girls basking nude at sandy beaches lapped by the blue Mediterranean near Saint-Tropez, the coast's legends

are still very real. But they are not the whole story.

The term Riviera usually includes not only the Mediterranean coast but the countryside behind, extending from around Cassis to the Italian border. The ribbons of golden sand disappearing into azure sea and the sheer, rocky spectacular views of the great Corniche routes between Nice and Monte Carlo attract obvious admiration, but less widely acclaimed sights wait to be discovered by adventurous travellers.

You can explore medieval villages—many now deserted, or

nearly so—perched perilously on their peaks, or clinging to their lofty outcrops like hazardous dice-throws. Cypresses and silvery olive groves, bright mimosa and roses, the heady wafts of thyme, rosemary and sage and the *garrigues,* the almost impenetrable scrub growth, are as much a part of southern France as the blue sea.

To really savour life down here try sitting in small-town squares. Take in the musically gurgling fountains and the desultory social life under the shade of outsized plane-trees, and learn how to relax.

The sun is out twice as much here as in Paris, even if out of season the climate is not always perfect. Winter has its share of cool or cold days, and any time of year the Mistral wind can come raging down the Rhône valley freshening the vivid hues of Provence, but also exhausting inhabitants and discouraging beach-goers with its incessant, irritating roar.

Given the bright colours and pervasive, luminous light, it's no wonder that artists since Fragonard have gravitated to the south. Monet, Matisse, Cocteau and Picasso are just a few who

celebrated the Riviera in unforgettable masterpieces.

Tourism is the area's largest business but not the only one. Other industries include shipbuilding, perfume, ceramics, glass and ready-to-wear garments. And the agricultural sector produces magnificent fruit and vegetables, olives, olive oil and wine for domestic consumption and for export.

Unfortunately, because of its success, this is not the place to find deserted beaches. The Riviera is thickly populated. Marseilles ranks as France's second largest city, and the number of people on the coast in the summer is almost double that of the rest of the year.

As for the natives of Provence, they have more in common with the easy-going, voluble Italians than with their cousins to the north. They speak in a drawn-out, lilting southern-French accent and there are several local

*Early morning—the time to beat the crowds at the Baie des Anges.*

dialects, or *patois,* which are difficult for outsiders to understand.

In fact, Provençal people act much like the characters in Marcel Pagnol's novels or the cinema star Fernandel. While genial smiles prevail, there is also a good deal of expressive eyeball-rolling, shoulder-shrugging and fist-waving. But the general mood is carefree, and you might as well sit back and forget schedules.

Just enjoy the good food and wine, the outgoing people, the beautiful scenery and glorious sunny weather that bless the French Riviera. For nowhere else will you find the unique blend that make this the world's most glamorous resort area.

*Delights of the back country—the charming square of Saint-Paul and bright yellow hillside.*

# A Brief History

The attractions of the French Riviera were discovered very early on. Artefacts have been found at Beaulieu, Nice and the Grimaldi Grottoes, indicating that people lived here in Palaeolithic and Neolithic times.

More definite history begins around 1,000 B.C. with the Ligurians, far-ranging colonizers from the south-east who settled along the coast. Four centuries later, the ubiquitous ships of Greece arrived and the Ligurians were forced to the east. These energetic Greek traders, the Phoceans, founded Marseilles, La Ciotat, Antibes and Nice. On two occasions, they called in Roman armies to help them fight the Ligurians.

Then in 125 B.C. the Romans marched in on their own account, determined to establish a passageway to their Iberian colony. They set up Provincia Narbonensis, which eventually became Provence. Among the important cities founded at this time were Narbonne, the capital, in 118 B.C., Aix in 123 B.C. and Fréjus in 49 B.C., built by Caesar as a rival to Marseilles.

The Greeks brought civilization and agriculture—the olive tree, the fig tree and grape vines—to the area; the Romans

introduced their administrative systems, law and agricultural methods. Roman influence lasted for nearly six centuries; and during this period of relative peace, roads, towns and cities burgeoned all over southern France.

## The Dark Ages

Christianity spread gradually throughout the Mediterranean during the first centuries A.D. In 450 the church of Provence was formally organized along the lines of Roman administration. Then hard times followed. From the 5th to 7th centuries, successive waves of invaders swept over the country, breaking down the established order and leaving behind an utter shambles.

The Franks, who created the basis of a French state, prevailed but Provence was left more or less autonomous until the rule of Charles Martel. In several campaigns between 736 and 739 he took Avignon, Marseilles and Arles, establishing his authority over the area. Charlemagne's reign (771-814) was one of relative stability, but his heirs squabbled over the domain. In 843, the empire was divided by treaty among Charlemagne's three grandsons: Provence fell to the lot of Lothaire I. When his son Charles assumed control in 855, it became the Kingdom of Provence.

From the 8th century on, the coast was often attacked by North African Moslems, known as Moors or Saracens. In 884, they even built a mountain base at La Garde-Freinet from which they swooped down to raid and pillage neighbouring communities. Before they were driven out almost a century later by Guillaume le Libérateur, the Saracens had forced many local overlords and their followers to retreat into the hills—the origin of the perched village strongholds that dot the Midi today.

## The Counts of Provence

The situation improved markedly in the 10th century. With the Saracens gone, the counts of Provence emerged as strong, independent rulers under the titular authority of the Holy Roman Empire. Trade and cultural activity revived. The 12th and 13th centuries were the heyday of the troubadours, the period when Provençal became the most important literary language of western Europe.

The counts of Barcelona gained title to Provence by a pro-

*La Garde-Freinet was once the base of the pillaging Saracens.*

## Langue d'Oc

An offshoot of Latin, Provençal began to take shape in the 4th century. By the 11th, it was widely spoken in the south, carried from Nice to Bordeaux by the troubadours. These roving ambassadors went from château to château, singing the praises of idealized love. Both in style and theme, their poetry influenced the development of Western literature.

The language was known as *occitan* because *oc* rather than the northern *oïl* (which became *oui*) was the word for "yes". After the 14th century *langue d'oc* started to break down into regional dialects. Then, in 1539, Francis I decreed that French should be used in all administrative matters, and that was really the end.

Today you may hear—but certainly not understand—a bit of Niçois, Monegasque or another vestige of Provençal. Some expressions, like *lou vieux mas* (the old farmhouse), have worked themselves into everyday life.

---

pitious marriage in 1112. One particularly able Catalonian ruler, Raimond Bérenger V, reorganized and unified the Comté de Provence. In 1246, his daughter Beatrix became the wife of Charles of Anjou (brother of Louis IX of France). The people of Provence received both commercial benefits and greater liberty from their ambitious new ruler who also became king of Naples and Sicily.

Avignon had its hour of glory in the 14th century. Through French influence, the bishop of Bordeaux was elected pope in 1305. The new pontiff, subservient to the kings of France, made Avignon rather than Rome his residence.

The ensuing period was a humiliating one for the Church but a golden age for Avignon. The city became a great cultural centre attracting many artists and scholars—notably Petrarch. It remained the religious capital until 1377, when Pope Gregory XI returned to Rome. But after his death, the "Great Schism" arose between Italian and French factions: there were two, and sometimes three popes (one in Avignon), each with his own College of Cardinals. The Schism did not come to an end until 1417.

### Provence Becomes French

After various changes of ruling powers, the larger part of Provence (including Aix and Marseilles) came back under the control of the Dukes of Anjou. The last of them, the civic- and artistic-minded "Good King René", left his domain to his nephew, who before dying 17 months later named Louis XI, King of France, his successor.

Thus Provence became part of France in 1481. Nice, however, went its separate way. It had formed an alliance with the Dukes of Savoy in 1388, and it remained Savoyard—with a few interruptions—until 1860.

The early 16th century was marked by strife between Francis I of France and Charles V, the Holy Roman Emperor. After an early victory in Milan (1515), the French monarch was driven out of Italy and imprisoned. Then it was the turn of Charles to invade Provence. In 1536, he took Aix and had himself crowned king of Arles before he was eventually checked at Marseilles and Arles and forced into a disastrous retreat.

Acting as go-between in 1538, Pope Paul III managed to get both sides to sign the Treaty of Nice, a precarious armistice at best. Never deigning to meet, each party convened separately with the pope in Nice. The truce didn't last.

In 1543, helped by the Turkish fleet, Francis I bombarded Nice (allied to his rival through the House of Savoy). After a valiant struggle, Nice repelled the invaders, returning to the realm of the House of Savoy.

## Wars and Revolutions

Meanwhile Europe had become the scene of fierce religious conflicts caused by the rise of Protestantism. The confrontations were especially bloody in the south of France. In 1545 more than 20 "heretic" villages (north of Aix) were levelled by order of Francis I; the years that followed saw much violence on both sides. The Edict of Nantes in 1598 palliated the situation by granting religious freedom to the Protestants (later revoked in 1685).

In the 17th century, Cardinal Richelieu, Louis XIII's all-powerful adviser, decided to reinforce the southern coast as protection against Spain. Following this, Toulon and Marseilles were converted into major ports. Measures of centralization and new taxes gave rise to much agitation and to outright rebellion, in the case of Marseilles. Louis XIV brought the troublesome city to heel in 1660, by imposing additional contributions and restrictions.

Provence was the battleground during the 17th and 18th centuries for numerous disputes, both domestic and foreign. France took and lost Nice several times but did gain some additional territory from the Duke of Savoy. A veritable disaster hit Provence in 1720: 100,000 people died in a great epidemic that was carried into Marseilles on a ship from the Middle East. **15**

Like the rest of France, Provence was profoundly affected by the revolution of 1789 and the cataclysmic upheavals that

*Man on the way up: Napoleon as portrayed by Baron Gros in 1796.*

followed. Bad crops and the election of a new Provençal Estates General contributed to the turbulence. Riots and massacres occurred in many places.

In the administrative reorganization of France in 1790, Provence was divided into three

*départements*—Var, Basses-Alpes, Bouches-du-Rhône—and violence continued.

Widespread reaction set in in 1794. Royalist extremists initiated the White Terror in Orange, Marseilles and Aix, slaughtering their Jacobin opponents. A state of lawlessness prevailed in some areas.

## Napoleon in the South

Profiting from the disarray, the English easily took Toulon in 1793. Napoleon Bonaparte, an obscure captain at the time, distinguished himself in the recapture of the city. Promoted to general, he launched his Italian campaign from Nice (annexed by France from 1793 to 1814) in 1796.

Two years later, Toulon was the starting-point for his sensational Egyptian campaign. When Napoleon returned in 1799, he landed triumphantly at Saint-Raphaël. You can see a small pyramid there erected to commemorate his victories.

However, his empire was unpopular in Provence, where Royalist sentiment remained strong. Besides, the Continental blockade was disastrous for Marseilles' trade, further exacerbating ill-feeling.

Napoleon went through Saint-Raphaël again in 1814—but this time in disgrace, ignominiously escorted by Austrian and Russian troops on his way to exile on Elba. He escaped from his island prison a year later, landing at Golfe-Juan and returning to Paris via Cannes, Grasse, Digne and Gap—a road now known as the Route Napoléon.

The Revolution of 1848 took the form of uprisings all over the south of France, as peasants demanded the right to land. They rebelled again in 1851 but were eventually quelled by government troops.

In 1860, the House of Savoy gave up Nice in return for Napoleon III's help in ousting the Austrians from the northern provinces of Italy. In a plebiscite, the Niçois overwhelmingly proclaimed their desire to join France. But Monaco stayed apart as a hereditary monarchy allied closely with France (see p. 41). In 1861, Monaco sold all rights to Menton and Roquebrune, which had also voted to join France.

## Twentieth Century

Southern France was scarcely concerned in the First World War, and the population east of Nice felt more drawn to the Italians than anybody else. It could not escape the Second World War, however. In 1940, the Italians opened hostilities against France and succeeded in **17** taking Menton. The Vichy government of Marshal Pétain was left to govern the rest of the area until the Germans took over at the end of 1942, with the Italians occupying the Côte d'Azur. But before the Germans arrived, the French scuttled their own fleet at Toulon, blocking that important harbour.

As the American, British and Allied forces approached from North Africa and Italy, the Germans put up blockhouses and barbed wire on the beaches; Saint-Tropez was dotted with mines and various beach obstacles. Then on August 15, 1944, the long-awaited landings began, led by General Patch's 7th Army. The Americans swarmed over the beach to Saint-Raphaël

*La Croisette, a favourite rendezvous for young and old at Cannes.*

and destroyed the blockhouses. The following day French General de Lattre de Tassigny landed with his Free French troops at Saint-Tropez. Within two weeks Provence was free.

The scars of war were quickly erased, and with the appearance of the bikini bathing costume (a Riviera original, in spite of the name), everyone took heart. Business started to skyrocket. So did a building and tourism boom, which hasn't stopped to this day.

## The Follies of Fashion

The English were the first to go to the Riviera. In the late 18th century, it was considered a fine place for consumptive and other fragile beings to escape the raw English winters. Summers, on the other hand, were shunned as being unbearably hot.

The English gravitated to Nice, especially Cimiez. Cannes was "discovered" in 1834 by Lord Brougham. Finally the French joined the sun seekers, when writers like George Sand, Alexandre Dumas and Guy de Maupassant became aware of the joys of the coast. Artists, writers, musicians, aristocrats and others followed. Every night of the winter season was brilliant with masked balls and assorted diversions.

The Riviera became a mecca for the Impressionists. Renoir and Cézanne loved the colour and light, as did the artists who arrived after them—Bonnard, Matisse, Léger and Picasso, to name but a few.

Towards the end of the 19th century, it was really the playground for international "high society", where royalty kissed the hands of American heiresses and French courtesans. The Russian aristocrats were legendary, travelling in private trains with dozens of servants.

The turn of America's affluent society came in the twenties. Charmed by the scenery and the low cost of a sybaritic life, millionaires and film stars started the vogue for the French coast in the summer.

Though the tone may have changed, people from all over still flock to the Riviera attracted by the aura of glamour and the sun.

# Where to Go

## Nice

*Pop 338,000*

Nice is like a rich dowager of simple origins who never lost her common touch. Unofficial capital of the Riviera, it is a vibrant, important city, boasting France's third largest airport, an opera house and excellent philharmonic orchestra, a university and several good museums. The city's shops, hotels and restaurants rival the world's best. However, the older quarters and their inhabitants have the theatrical, good-natured, brawling character of an Italian town.

Greeks (Phoceans) from Marseilles settled here in the 4th century B.C., and the name Nice may have come from *nike*, the Greek word for victory. Two centuries later, Romans left the seaport to fishermen and built a town on the Cimiez hill.

Nice broke away from the rest of Provence in 1388, when it was annexed by the House of Savoy. In the following century, the hill now known as Le Château supported a fortified castle, and beneath it a city grew up (now the *vieille ville*).

In 1631, Nice was almost wiped out by the plague—but it survived. Bonaparte used the city as a base during his Italian campaign. It joined France officially in 1860.

Although Nice was known as a winter resort in the late 1700s, its touristic career really got underway in the next century with the arrival of the English and their queen, Victoria.

### Promenade des Anglais

Any visit to Nice passes along this splendid palm-tree-lined 5 kilometre long boulevard. It starts in the east outside the airport and the spectacular ultra-modern hotel and business complex of Arenas. Next door is the exotic flower-filled Phoenix Park containing the largest single-span glasshouse in the world (7,000m²/75,000ft²).

For most of the way the Promenade—thus named because in the 1820's the widening of a narrow coastal path was paid for by local English residents—runs beside the Mediterranean shoreline (with both public and private beaches) of the Baie des Anges. Half way along is the legendary Negresco —a stunning Belle Epoque hotel with an imposing rococo facade, colourful turrets and costumed doormen. The Negresco's Chantecler Restaurant is reputed to be one of the finest in Europe.

At the end of the promenade where it joins the Quai des Etats-Unis and Le Chateau—the rock

that cuts off Nice from its harbour—is a flowered park, the **Jardin Albert-Ier**, with an 18th-century Triton fountain and a modern outdoor theatre. Behind the gardens, running parallel to the Promenade des Anglais, are "shopping streets", mostly reserved for pedestrians.

On the other side of the park is the Place Masséna, a picturesque square of arcaded buildings in ruddy stucco, built in 1835.

## La Vieille Ville

You can enter the old city from the seaside (Quai des Etats-Unis) or the Place Masséna. From this latter direction, you'll pass the **Opéra** and its elaborate 19th-century façade. On the **Cours Saleya** (the name comes from "salt", which was at one time sold in bulk here), you shouldn't miss the flower market, open from 6 a.m. to 4 p.m., full of the colour and the scent of roses, tulips, dahlias and geraniums. Also on the Cours Saleya, the fruit and vegetable market takes place from 6 a.m. to 1 p.m. and is just as picturesque, though more aromatic. Both markets are open daily except Monday when there is an antique and bric-à-brac market from 8 a.m. to 4 p.m.

On the quay side, the little pastel houses where fishermen used to live (mostly restaurants and art galleries now) are known as *ponchettes,* a provençal word meaning little rocks. Opposite is the **Miséricorde** chapel. Built by the Black Penitents (a lay sect) in 1736, it contains an attractive altar-piece by Miralhet, *La Vierge de la Miséricorde.*

Turning left at the end of the Cours Saleya, you'll enter the old world of Nice with its appetizing aromas, tiny shops spilling their wares onto the streets, excited voices talking Niçois, a form of Provençal that rolls like Italian. **Rue Droite** just looks like a cramped alleyway now, but it was the main street in the Middle Ages. On the right is Saint-Jacques, the heavily decorated baroque church modelled after Il Gesù in Rome. Set back on the left is Sainte-Réparate cathedral (1650) with its handsome 18th-century belfry.

Showcase of the old town, the **Palais Lascaris** (15, rue Droite) is a 17th-century town house that belonged to the Lascaris family of Ventimiglia until the French Revolution. Guided tours of historical Nice begin here daily at 3 p.m. (Mondays excepted). Small for a palace, the building has a handsome carved marble staircase and frescoed ceilings; don't miss the odd-angled carved door,

*A superb sampling of molluscs and crustaceans served at seafood bar.*

built to swing shut automatically. On the ground floor is a beautifully preserved pharmacy, dating from 1738, complete with apothecary jars. The whole shop came from Besançon, a gift of the Gould family (American industrialists).

Further on you'll find Place Saint-François with its nicely proportioned, late-baroque, former town hall. Every morning except Monday, a frenetic fish market takes over the square—gleaming with red mullet, sea bass and squid.

On Place Garibaldi, just outside the old town, a handsome Calder stabile stands in front of the bus station. Esplanade Kennedy, nearby, is the site of the Acropolis, Nice's exhibition and conference centre.

## Le Château and the Harbour

Though you won't find anything left of Nice's stronghold of the Middle Ages, destroyed in 1706, a visit to the 300-foot summit of Le Château is pleasant nonetheless. Hardy walkers can climb the steps in 15 minutes, but a lift service also operates from 9 a.m. to 6 p.m. daily from the Quai des Etats-Unis. A more popular way of seeing Le Château is to take the "little white train" which runs from Quai des Etats-Unis through the Cours Saleya and the narrow streets of the old town. It is in service throughout the year except from January 1 to the start of Carnival Week in February. It runs every 20 minutes from 10 a.m. to 7 p.m. daily except Mondays, when it starts at 2 p.m. It is a highly enjoyable experience, especially if you leave the train at the top (it turns round and comes straight back), take in the views, have a drink in the café and come down by a later train.

At the top there is a public park, with exotic pines and cacti—and a spectacular view of the colourful port on one side and the Baie des Anges on the other. The white stones you'll see are remnants of Romanesque religious buildings. Military buffs will be interested by the naval museum in the Tour Bellenda (closed Tuesday).

Filled with pleasure and merchant boats, the port is always lively—lined with bars, cafés and restaurants specializing in the Niçois version of the famous Mediterranean fish stew—bouillabaisse. From the northeast corner of the harbour, you can take the Boulevard Carnot to an extraordinary museum, the **Terra Amata,** at number 25. Practically hidden under towering residential buildings, it contains a

*Shop talk is just part of the fun on this pedestrian mall in Nice.*

sizeable collection of prehistoric remains found when the land was being cleared for construction. Three hundred thousand years ago, the sea reached 85 feet higher than today, and primitive men hunted on the shores which now lie under these buildings.

### Cimiez

Originally built by the Romans, this hilly residential suburb was much favoured by the European aristocracy during the 19th century. Grandest of the many hotels and villas constructed at that time is the former Hôtel Excelsior Régina Palace—a favourite of Queen Victoria that was later converted into apartments. Matisse spent his later life in one of these.

Within easy reach of Nice city centre (you can take bus no. 15 from Place Masséna), the route to Cimiez passes close to the Chagall Museum at the lower end of Boulevard Cimiez. At the top of the boulevard is the Régina Palace and Villa des Arènes, the latter containing an archeological museum and the Matisse museum. Important works from all periods of

Matisse's life are displayed with personal objects from his studio.

Behind the villa you can walk around the Roman ruins (from the 2nd and 3rd centuries A.D.), including the remains of a small amphitheatre and part of the Roman bath complex. The ruins are open from 10 a.m. to noon and 2.30 to 6.30 p.m. (summer), 5 p.m. (winter). Closed Sunday morning and all day Monday.

On the eastern side is a Franciscan monastery with a late Gothic church (extensively restored in the 17th century) containing three remarkable alterpieces painted on wood in the 15th century by Ludovico Bréa. Open 10 a.m. to noon and 3 to 5 p.m., closed over the weekend. Both Matisse and Dufy are buried in the adjoining cemetery.

*Wriggling whitebait fresh from the sea; below: the imposing ruins of Roman baths at Cimiez.*

## Nice Excursions

Nice is an excellent starting point for short tours all along the Riviera and for some out-of-the-ordinary trips into the area behind Nice.

If you enjoy spectacular scenery and mountain driving, take the day-long tour featuring the twin gorges of Daluis and Cians. Leaving Nice on RN 202 you will follow the River Var and pass through numerous medieval villages. ENTREVAUX – a perfectly preserved fortified town with drawbridge, ramparts and hilltop citadel – is well worth a visit. Then head for Guillaumes via the grandiose Gorges de Daluis, outstanding for their depth and red schist colouring. Stops then include the ski resort of VALBERG and the old Alpine town of BEUIL before entering the **Gorges du Cians**, where the river plunges 1600m/5250ft as it flows into the Var.

Another spectacular excursion goes to the **Vésubie Valley**— green mountain slopes and rushing waters fed by melting snows. Visit SAINT-MARTIN-VÉSUBIE, located on a spur between two torrential streams that form the Vésubie. Nearby, at the Mercantour National Park, don't miss the beautiful **Vallée des Merveilles** (open July to October) with its prehistoric rock engravings.

The sinuous road leading up to the **Madone d'Utelle** (3,850 feet) passes by an interesting 18th century church in UTELLE. At the summit you'll find a breathtaking view and a sanctuary founded in 850 (rebuilt in 1806).

# The Corniches

The pre-Alpine mountains between Nice and Menton drop to the sea in a changing panorama of spectacular scenery.

The highest views are from the route known as the **Grande Corniche,** built by Napoleon along the ancient Aurelian Way. The **Moyenne** (middle) **Corniche** offers a contrast of rocky cliffs and the sea. The **Corniche Inférieure,** or Corniche du Littoral, runs along beside the sea and can be terribly crowded in summer but some very worthwhile places are located on this road. Six kilometres east of Nice, **Villefranche** is one of the most sheltered Mediterranean harbours.

Clinging to a steep slope under the road, Villefranche offers instant charm, with its yellow, pink and red stucco or brick

*The colourful Villefranche quay is fine for fishing or a picnic.*

houses packed against the hill, the plunging alleyways and staircases and the covered **Rue Obscure** that snakes down to the sea. The quayside cafés are well placed for watching the pleasure boats and for a view of Cap Ferrat, pointing off to the left like a green finger.

On the right, below the town's old citadel (built for the Duke of Savoy in 1560), is the 14th-century Chapelle Saint-Pierre, also known as the **Cocteau chapel,** since writer-artist Jean Cocteau decorated it in 1956. The pastel, boldly outlined drawings completely fill the small vaulted chapel with scenes of fishermen, plus biblical episodes from the life of St. Peter.

A short drive around the rocky, pine-green peninsula of **Cap Ferrat** will convince you that the rich indeed appreciate privacy. The view is mostly of gates hinting of grandeur. The vast, cream-coloured villa that belonged to King Leopold II of the Belgians can only be seen from afar. Somerset Maugham lived in Villa Mauresque, also rather well hidden.

The best views are from the upper levels of the **Ephrussi de Rothschild** foundation, also known as Musée Ile-de-France. Built between 1905–12 by Madame Béatrice Ephrussi, née Rothschild, the pinkish Italian-style villa is the delirious assemblage of an insatiable art collector. While you'll see a Coromandel screen and other beautiful *chinoiseries,* as well as examples of Renaissance, Louis XIII furniture and a few Impressionist paintings, the museum really shines in its French 18th century pieces. The collection of Sèvres porcelain, composed of thousands of rare pieces and signed complete sets, is perhaps the largest in the world. The gardens surrounding the villa are no less extraordinary: the main one is French style, but bordered by others of worldwide inspiration. The house and gardens are closed Sunday morning, all day Monday and November.

Not far away, the modest Cap Ferrat zoo offers an unlikely contrast. Favourite with children are the trained monkey shows (*Ecole des chimpanzés*).

SAINT-JEAN-CAP-FERRAT is the port side of the peninsula, with a modern seaside promenade and an older fishing village; Cocteau decorated the marriage room of its small town hall.

Beaulieu—a favourite Riviera resort with the English during the last century—is today an elegant seaside town enjoying one of the mildest climates of the entire coast. There is a bustling fruit and vegetable market every morning in the main square and popular quayside bars and restaurants surround Beaulieu's crowded marina.

Of particular interest is Villa Kérylos which is one of the few great villas of the Riviera open to the public. Built by scholar-musician-bibliophile Théodore Reinach in the early 20th century, it is acknowledged as the finest recreation of an authentic Greek villa in the world. Designed to be a perfect replica in every detail, it is constructed

*Ephrussi de Rothschild museum, a pink palace on Cap Ferrat.*

from marble, alabaster and exotic woods. Many Ancient Greek antiques—vases, statuettes, mosaics etc—have been incorporated into the overall design.

Villa Kérylos is open every afternoon except Mondays and is closed throughout November and the first week of December.

The Grande Corniche road goes all the way to Menton (via Roquebrune and the Vistaëro lookout). You can stop off at La Turbie, or explore the higher roads, visiting villages like PEILLE and PEILLON.

On a clear day, the **Belvédére d'Eze** (1,680 ft.) offers a panoramic view of the coast, the Tête de Chien mountain over Monte Carlo, the old perched city of Eze below and, on the right, as far as Cap d'Antibes and the Estérel mountains.

LA TURBIE's star curiosity is the **Trophée des Alpes,** a round ruin with Doric columns standing guard over Monaco. Emperor Augustus built it in 6 B.C. to celebrate victory over various battling peoples who had prevented the construction of a road between Rome and Gaul.

Highlight of the Moyenne Corniche (best road of the three) is the village of **Eze.** It hangs at a dizzying angle above the sea—majestic and deep blue from this perspective. One of the most magnificent views on the coast. Medieval Eze is closed to traffic but not tourists who flock here in all seasons. On the site of an old château, razed in 1706 by Louis XIV, is a public garden full of exotic flowers and cacti. Amble around the narrow stone streets filled with souvenir shops.

CORNICHES

Continuing on, the Moyenne Corniche skirts around Monaco (see p. 37). Enjoy the stunning view at CABBÉ before turning off for Roquebrune and Menton. Instead of **Roquebrune** ("brown rock"), the town should really have been called "Roquerose"— for pink is what you see here on a sunny day (caused by reflections from the sienna-red stucco buildings along the streets). You can visit the dungeon of the fortified castle, built in the 10th century by a count of Ventimiglia to fend off the Saracens. Stony and spartan, the ruin still looks very much the fortress, with walls 6 to 12 feet thick and a bedroom furnished with a blunderbuss. A hole plunging hundreds of feet down was just what it looks like—a toilet!

Part of the Roquebrune municipality, the CAP MARTIN promontory is a millionaire's enclave, green with pine and olive trees, favoured in the last century when nobody cared much for sea-bathing (there is no beach).

Hot-point of the Riviera for climate, lukewarm for fun and games, **Menton** is a favourite of retired people for its warmth, simplicity and two casinos (the main one is a baroque gem).

*Witness to the past: a narrow medieval street in Roquebrune.*

Lemons flourish in this sunny spot. In February there is a lemon festival—the 15 or so tons of citrus fruits used in the décor are later sent to hospitals or made into jam. Menton is also proud of its olives and *clémentines*. It's no surprise that the natives like to tell their Adam-and-Eve legend: when they were chased from Paradise, Eve took along a lemon. After finding this new garden very like Paradise, she planted the "immortal fruit", which sprang up all over the slopes under the greyish lime.

A long pebble beach and Promenade George V lead to a

16th century bastion, now a **Cocteau museum;** further along is a jetty with a lighthouse and the modern Garavan harbour. You can see how the old town crowds up from the sea.

Every Friday from 7.30 a.m. to 5 p.m. there is an antique market at the **Place aux Herbes,** with its arcades and three huge plane trees. From there you can go uphill to reach the heart of the **old town,** which has a decidedly

*Happily dozing in its sun-warmed setting, Menton attracts young yachtsmen and seasoned sailors.*

Italian air. Here the 17th century church of **Saint-Michel** occupies a charming square with a view right to Italy. Cocteau painted some bold and fanciful allegorical frescoes in the marriage room of the Hôtel de Ville (town hall). The Musée Municipal contains odd bits of folklore, modern works and old bones, though not the famed pre-historic Grimaldi man once exhibited here.

Two public gardens in Menton are worth a look. The **Jardin**

*Rocky hike around Sainte-Agnès, highest of the perched villages.*

**Botanique,** arranged around a villa called Val Rahmeh, proves that everything can indeed grow in Menton—from a riot of roses to Mexican yucca, fuchsia and Japanese cane bamboo.

More curious is the **Jardin des Colombières.** Built by writer-painter Ferdinand Bac, the Hellenic-style villa (now converted into a modest hotel-restaurant) sits in the midst of Mediterranean lushness—with a splendid view. The terraced gardens out back are a romantic haven of flowered walks, punctuated by cypresses, ponds, fountains and statuary.

Around Menton, hikers can venture up through groves of gnarled olive trees, pine and scrub oak and finally the thick *maquis,* or bushy growth, scented with wild herbs.

Picturesque sites just a short drive away include SAINTE-AGNÈS, which claims to be the highest of the local perched villages; L'ANNONCIADE, a Capuchin monastery with a beautiful view; and the picturesque medieval towns of GORBIO and CASTELLAR.

If you long for real Italian spaghetti, just cross the border to **Ventimiglia.** A visit here should include the Romanesque cathedral, the baptistery (11th century) and a walk through the old streets.

# Monaco
*Pop. 30,000*

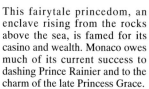

This fairytale princedom, an enclave rising from the rocks above the sea, is famed for its casino and wealth. Monaco owes much of its current success to dashing Prince Rainier and to the charm of the late Princess Grace.

The atmosphere here is both big city and miniature operatic. There are always crowds in this paradise, which has a population density comparable to Hong Kong's and cars jamming thoroughfares all over the hills (use the public lifts which take passengers effortlessly up). But the smartly uniformed Monegasque *gendarmes* keep order, and the streets are the cleanest on the Riviera.

Don't get the idea that gambling is the only local attraction; a mere 5 per cent of the principality's revenue comes from the casino. Many other commercial and cultural activities take precedence. For one thing, Monaco is a music capital with a top European orchestra and ballet company, an opera house and a music festival. Then there's the motor rally and the Grand Prix, synonymous with the name Monte Carlo, which set the sinuous streets roaring. Besides brilliant galas and balls, Monaco **37** holds a dog show, flower show and TV festival. It also boasts a good soccer team and a radio station that beams all over Europe. Last but not least, philatelists know of Monaco's beautiful stamps.

To clarify nomenclature: Monaco refers to the principality, geographically the historic peninsula-rock where you'll see the palace; Monte Carlo (which means Mount Charles) is the newer 19th century area curving out east of the rock. In between lies La Condamine, a land-fill flat area, comprising the harbour and modern business district. There is also a fourth district, Fontvieille, which is a new town built on reclaimed land to the west of The Rock.

## Monte Carlo

All roads lead to the main **casino** (and opera), introduced by a neatly tended garden-promenade. Any resemblance to the Paris Opéra is more than coincidental, since architect Charles Garnier designed both.

A busily decorated foyer with frescoes and bosomy caryatides in 19th century style take you in to the opera. Off to the left are the gambling rooms. If you can tear your eyes away from the roulette wheels, the ornate décor here is a delight. Especially amusing is the Salon Rose, where painted, unclad nymphs float about the ceiling smoking cigarillos.

Next door stands the **Hôtel de Paris,** an equally opulent historical monument. Louis XIV's bronze horse in the entrance hall has so often been "stroked for luck" by gamblers that its extended fetlock shines like gold. The dining room has been brilliantly redecorated in Louis XV style and is the first restaurant in Monaco to be awarded three Michelin stars.

Across the square, you'll find the lively Café de Paris, a crowded rendez-vous that hums with the frantic whir of slot machines, helpfully installed for the use of gambling addicts between drinks.

Nearby, Monaco's **National Museum** contains a delightful doll museum! Also known as the Musée Galéa, this whimsical spot houses a 2,000-piece collection assembled by Madeleine de Galéa. The villa-museum designed by Charles Garnier is a pink confection, perfect as a doll's house, nestled in a garden that has statues by Rodin, Maillol and Bourdelle. Exhibits include tableaux and exquisitely

*Monte Carlo's star attraction—its baroque casino-opera house.*

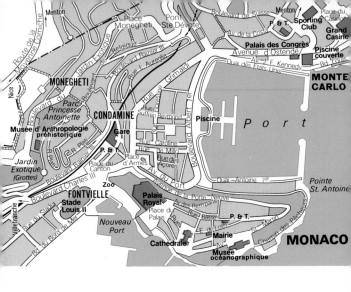

outfitted dolls from the 18th century to modern models. A series of automatons perform when the guard winds them up; there are extraordinary "acts" by mechanical card-players, acrobats, dancers and a snake-charmer—slightly spooky but quite impressive. Children love it.

### The Monaco Rock

A short ride up the hill from the centre of town, you'll find the Palais du Prince (bus or taxi recommended; parking space is severely limited).

The Grimaldis still live here, but you can visit the palace from June to the middle of October. The tour includes a look at the magnificent 17th century interior courtyard with its double marble staircase and painted gallery, **Galerie d'Hercule.** There are several well-maintained rooms containing priceless antiques, a gallery of mirrors, paintings by Van Loo, Brueghel and Titian, royal family portraits and the elaborate bed where the Duke of York died in 1767.

Any time of the year, at 11.55 a.m., you can watch the changing of the guard outside the palace. With fife and drums, much circumstance and little pomp, it's

## The Grimaldis

Monaco's past is sensational—full of intrigues and murder in high places. By a tortuous path, it arrived at the present constitutional monarchy under the personal rule of Prince Rainier III.

The rock of Monaco was inhabited from the Stone Age onwards. In 1215, the Genoese built a fortress there, which the Guelf and Ghibelline factions disputed for the rest of the century. Finally in 1297, the Guelfs led by François Grimaldi gained the upper hand. The Grimaldi family has hung on tenaciously ever since.

Treaties with powerful neighbours assured Monaco's independence over the years (except for a French interlude from 1793 to 1814). Roquebrune and Menton broke off from the principality in 1848 and were later bought by France. Looking for a new source of revenue, Monaco's ruler, Charles III, founded the Société des Bains de Mer in 1861 to operate gambling facilities. The venture got off to a slow start, but when François Blanc, a financial and administrative wizard with a shady background, took over, business prospered. On Blanc's advice, Charles commissioned the construction of a casino and opera house.

Hotels went up, and a railway line from the rest of the coast was soon extended to Monaco. A new (though perilous) coach-road and word-of-mouth publicity brought gamblers and fun-seekers.

In spite of tricky legal tangles, Monaco has retained its independent (and tax-free!) status, with open boundaries to France, free currency exchange (French money is almost always used) and a common post-telephone system with France.

Monaco is a nice place to live but it's almost impossible to become a citizen—unless you can find some Monegasque ancestors.

a good five minutes' worth of entertainment—though hardly up to Buckingham Palace standards.

The **old town** is also located on the Monaco Rock. Along the narrow pedestrian streets riddled with souvenir shops, restaurants and other tourist attractions, a gay atmosphere prevails, ringing with the Italian inflections of Monegasque *patois*.

On Rue Basse, you'll come across **L'Historial des Princes de Monaco**—a quaint wax museum assembled in 1971 by a Frenchman who likes Monaco.

From the earliest Grimaldi, François, to the youngest, Princess Stéphanie, the beautifully costumed personages present a pleasant historical panorama.

The cathedral is a white, 19th-century neo-Romanesque monster, boasting a tryptich by Louis Bréa (right transept). Behind the high altar is the burial place of Princess Grace.

**Musée Océanographique** is a formidable, grey-pillared construction, founded in 1910 by Prince Albert I, who spent the better part of his time at sea. It is now directed by Commandant Jacques-Yves Cousteau, the underwater explorer. In the basement aquarium, playful sea lions, jaded turtles and thousands of small incandescent fish cavort. Bear in mind the 50F entry charge which makes it the most expensive museum to visit on the coast.

The **Jardin Exotique** above the Condamine is worth visiting for the good view of the principality (take the lift from the port). Stepping stones lead you through a display of exotic plants—especially fierce-looking

spiny cacti in thousands of varieties, from South America and Africa.

Near the entrance to the Jardin Exotique is the **Anthropological Museum** *(Musée d'Anthropologie Préhistorique)*, where you'll see old bones from Menton and Monaco caves, plus ancient jewellery found in the Condamine. The 250 steps leading down to the *grottes* will reward you with a cool promenade through lacy pinpoints of stalactites and stalagmites.

Not far off is the **Stade Louis-II,** one of Europe's biggest sports complexes, and the Princess Grace Rose Garden.

*Monaco is both a bustling high-rise city and a seaside resort.*

There's also a zoo—small, friendly but unspectacular, bar a good view.

If you just want to relax go to **Larvotto Beach**. This is a top quality man-made beach with imported sand, trees, shower facilities and a selection of bars and restaurants. It is also free.

# Nice to Cannes

In all respects, this is one of the richest areas of the Riviera. The scenery can be magnificent, and art works abound both along the coast and in the villages behind.

### Côte d'Antibes

Founded by the Phoceans in the 4th century B.C., **Antibes** got its name (Antipolis—the "city opposite") because it faced Nice across the Baie des Anges. The first landmark you'll see here is the imposing square fortress, **Fort Carré**. This was the French kings' stronghold against the dukes of Savoy who controlled Nice. In 1794, Napoleon lodged his family here while supervising the coastal defence. Since he wasn't very well paid, his sisters filched figs and artichokes from neighbouring farmers. Today the hills around Antibes are lined with glassy greenhouses; growing flowers is the main local industry.

Don't miss a tour around the ramparts, reconstructed by Vauban in the 17th century along the original medieval lines. The **Château Grimaldi,** now the Musée Picasso, is a white stone castle with a Romanesque tower built by the lords of Antibes on a Roman site. Besides many classical relics, the museum possesses a rich Picasso collection. In 1946, when the artist was having difficulty finding a place to work, the director of Antibes' museum offered him the premises as a studio. Picasso set to work among the dusty antiquities. Inspired by the classical objects around him, he completed over 145 works in a period of six months. The grateful artist gave these drawings, ceramics, paintings and other pieces from a later period to the museum.

Next to the château-museum is a 17th century **church** with a Romanesque apse and transept and an altarpiece attributed to Louis Bréa. Behind the sunny square you'll find a maze of old streets and the covered market, colourful in the morning when it's in full swing.

Just around the bay lies the **Cap d'Antibes,** a quiet, pine-covered peninsula well endowed with big, beautiful houses and a venerable hotel, the Eden-Roc. It served as a model for F. Scott Fitzgerald, and today you can

usually see film stars and magnates lolling around its pool poised high above the sea.

The **Chapelle Notre-Dame** at LA GAROUPE is of curious composition: one nave is 13th century, the other 16th and each is dedicated to a different madonna. They are both filled with ex-votos, all kinds of naïve arts works or objects offered as prayers of thanks. Around the western side of the cape is the sandy crescent-shaped bay of

*Watchful portrait of Picasso hangs in the museum among his own works.*

JUAN-LES-PINS. The resort enjoyed its heyday in the twenties and thirties after American tycoon Frank Jay Gould built a big hotel and casino in a pinewood setting. Sleepy in winter, the town becomes rather wild in summer with a gaudy atmosphere generated by nightclubs, **45** cafés, boutiques spilling their wares into the streets and a restless, funseeking crowd of young people.

The artisans' towns of Vallauris and Biot are only a few minutes' drive from Antibes. **Vallauris** is inevitably associated with Picasso, who worked here after the war, giving new impetus to a dying ceramics and pottery industry. He presented the town with the bronze statue, *Man with a Sheep,* on Place Paul-Isnard and decorated the Romanesque chapel there, now the National Picasso Museum, with the **murals** *War and Peace.*

Careful buyers still find worthwhile purchases in the ceramics shops that line Vallauris' one main street.

Perched on a cone-shaped hill, **Biot** also bulges with artisans' shops and has a restored Romanesque church (too dark most of the time to see a fine Bréa altarpiece) and a colourful 13th century square with fountains and arcades.

Downhill, in the Biot glassworks you can see craftsmen dressed in shorts fashioning the heavy, tinted glass with minute bubbles that the town is known for.

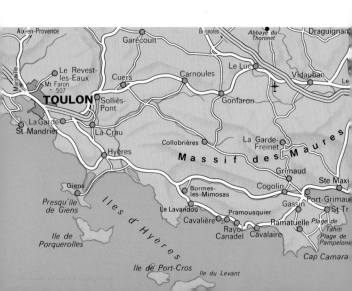

Adjacent to Biot, the **Musée National Fernand Léger** with its bold façade stands out like a giant postage stamp from miles away. Light and airy inside, the modern structure, built and donated to France by the artist's widow, houses an incomparable collection of Léger's works—from paintings to enormous tapestries.

Children like the dolphin show at Marineland near Biot railway station, while food buffs will be interested in the Museum of Culinary Art at VILLENEUVE-LOUBET, the birthplace of chef Auguste Escoffier.

## Inland Route

Spread out over hills covered with orange and olive trees, CAGNES-SUR-MER is not one but three towns: the seaside resort of CROS-DE-CAGNES, the modern commercial section of LE LOGIS and the ancient hilltop fortress, **Haut-de-Cagnes**—the prettiest and most interesting part. Its narrow, cobbled streets corkscrew up to the **castle.** To enter, you pass through an ivy-covered, oblique-angled patio with galleries all around and a huge pepper tree in the centre. On the ground floor of the castle visit a curious museum devoted to

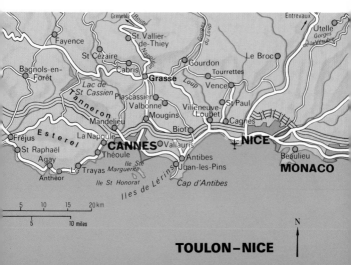

TOULON–NICE

olives—their history, cultivation, literature—probably the greatest tribute ever paid to that fruit.

Upstairs are exhibits of contemporary art and a ceremonial hall with a splendid 17th century *trompe-l'œil* ceiling, *The Fall of Phaeton*. One extraordinary room contains 40 portraits of Suzy Solidor, the one-time cabaret queen, as seen by famous 20th century painters—from a doe-eyed girl wearing a sailor suit by Van Dongen to a raffish, much older version of her wearing a matador's hat.

Renoir spent his last years (1907-19) in the villa of Les Collettes just east of Cagnes. However, there's not much left to see here besides mementoes and a few of the master's minor works.

**Saint-Paul-de-Vence** is another venerable bastion, built within spade-shaped walls and looming over what were once green terraces of vineyards, mimosa and cypress trees, now a parade of elegant country villas in lush gardens.

The walled feudal city, entered by foot under a tower and arch with a cannon pointing right at you, was built by Francis I in the 16th century as a defence against Nice and the dukes of Savoy.

Under the big plane trees of the Place du Général-de-Gaulle, you'll usually find a lively game of *pétanque* (or *boules*), the outdoor bowling game played with leaded balls. The Colombe d'Or hotel across the street has an important private collection of modern art, acquired from the likes of Picasso, Leger and Calder in exchange for meals in the restaurant.

You can make the tour of the narrow pedestrian streets in a few minutes or at a leisurely pace with stops at the Grande Fontaine and Gothic church.

On a wooded hill just outside Saint-Paul is one of the great modern art museums of the world—the **Fondation Maeght,** inaugurated in 1964 by Paris art dealer Aimé Maeght and his wife. The museum sits in a green grove of dark pines. Full of visual surprises, the brick-steel-glass construction designed by Spanish-American architect José Luis Sert is an ideal place for displaying modern art. The permanent collection, including paintings and lithographs by many of the great names of 20th century art, is packed away in summer to make room for a temporary show. Any time of year you can see the superb sculpture **49**

*Special sights on Côte d'Azur—a stunning sunrise and potter at work in artisan town of Vallauris.*

collection, featuring many fine Mirós and Giacomettis.

**Vence** is an ancient bishopric with middle-age spread: the charming old city has been girdled by newer shops and houses. English and French artists and retired people like the bustling atmosphere, the surrounding hills and the peace that falls at night (off-season, of course!).

In the 17th century, the remarkable Antoine Godeau became bishop of Vence. A mis-shapen society wit, he turned to the holy orders at the age of 30, undertook restoration of the cathedral, founded new industries to give work to his parishioners and was appointed one of the first members of the august Académie Française.

*A ramble through the old town of Tourrettes is always rewarding; opposite: Grasse flower market.*

The best scenic points of old Vence are the **Place du Peyra** with its gurgling fountain and friendly cafés, the cathedral (especially the arresting Romanesque belfry), and the **Place du Frêne** with a centuries-old ash tree whose trunk must be at least 6 feet in diameter.

Tourists often hurry past Vence on their way to the **Chapelle du Rosaire-Henri Matisse** on the road to Saint-Jeannet (only open to the public on certain days, see p. 80). Dedicated by Matisse to the Dominican nuns who cared for him during a long illness, the chapel is the crowning achievement of the artist, then in his eighties and practically blind. The famed stained-glass windows in bold patterns of royal blue, bright green and yellow give radiant light to the simple chapel, two walls of which are decorated by powerful line-drawing figures on white faïence.

A short tour of the **Loup Valley** is worthwhile and will take you less than a day. Highlights include TOURRETTES, a charming old town popular with artisans and artists, several waterfalls (Cascade de Courmes, Cascade des Demoiselles) and the town of GOURDON, built on a steep spur 2,500 feet high. The castle here was a Saracen fort in

the 9th century and contains a small medieval museum.

**Grasse,** the world's perfume capital, won't knock you over with heady scents; but you can't miss the enormous signs inviting you to visit the factories.

Although the Grassois were distilling essential essences from **51** local flowers as far back as the 13th century, the industry didn't bloom until the Medici family launched the fashion of scented gloves in the 16th century (Grasse made gloves as well).

Nowadays the manufacturers use at least 10,000 tons of flowers—violets (January to March), mimosa (February), daffodil (April), rose and orange-flowers and so on—to produce their essence. The gleaming brass cauldrons, alembics and other trappings displayed in the factories, though mainly for show, do give an idea of the first steps in making perfume and soap. The high price of perfume becomes understandable when you realize it takes a ton of petals to produce just 2.2 pounds of essence. The attractive soaps and scents on sale here have little to do with the sophisticated Paris-made brands, which use the Grasse essences in carefully guarded formulas.

Built on a steep hill, Grasse was already renowned for its good air in the 19th century, and invalids and people on holiday flocked here. The most charming spot in town is the friendly, crowded **Place aux Aires,** with its fountains, arcades and sculptured 18th century façades. The morning market is a palette of brilliant colours (flowers and vegetables) under the blue shade of lotus *(micocoulier)* and plane trees.

A few blocks downhill, the Place aux Herbes has an even larger food market. Several steps away is the sober, ochrestone **cathedral,** begun in the 12th century and restored in the 17th. Inside you'll find cradle-vaulting and a rare religious canvas by Honoré Fragonard, *The Washing of the Feet.*

The **Musée Fragonard,** on the Boulevard Fragonard, occupies the villa where the painter spent a year during the French Revolution. He brought with him a series of love-scene paintings which had been turned down by Madame du Barry. Most of the collection had ended up in the Frick Museum in New York,

*Perfumes come in many hues at Gourdon; right: a cool sail on the artificial lake of Saint-Cassien.*

but the excellent and sensuous **Three Graces** remains.

**Musée d'Art et d'Histoire de Provence** in the Rue Mirabeau is housed in an elegant 18th century town house once owned by the Marquise de Cabris. Her furniture is in remarkably good condition. Among the less conventional articles on display are a nicely carved wooden bidet-chair with shell-shaped basin and a pewter bathtub on wheels.

Grasse is a good starting point for delightful side trips. Gourdon and the Loup Valley (see p. 51) are off to the north-east; to the south-west you have the Tanneron range and the man-made lake of Saint-Cassien, a popular place for windsurfing.

CABRIS (6 km. on the D4 road) commands an impressive view from its old château ruins—the Tanneron hills, the Esterel and La Napoule to the right, Mougins and the Lérins Islands to the left; and on a clear day you can even make out the hazy outline of Corsica.

Another 8 kilometres or so further on, the GROTTES DE SAINT-CÉZAIRE provide refreshing respite from the sun with stalactite shapes in extraordinary dark-red and pink colours. SAINT-CÉZAIRE itself is a peaceful, pretty town with a Romanesque chapel and a good view. You can continue north through wild, rocky limestone hills with low trees and bushes, up to MONS (32 km. from Grasse), an ancient perched village, to the COL DE VALFERRIÈRE, and back down the Route Napoléon through SAINT-VALLIER and several splendid panoramas.

Or you may want to continue west into the Var, visiting typical towns like FAYENCE (27 km. from Grasse), BARGEMON (44 km.), DRAGUIGNAN (56 km.) and perhaps the **Abbaye du Thoronet** (two hours' drive from Grasse). Lost in a beautiful landscape of reddish bauxite and green pine scrub trees, it's a cool, quiet place. The pink-stoned Thoronet, one of the three great abbeys of Provence, dates from the 12th century. It is notable for its clean-lined simplicity, its squat, colonnaded cloister and a hexagonal fountain, the *lavabo,* where the monks used to bathe.

# Cannes
*Pop. 68,000*

During the film festival in May and the record festival (MIDEM) in January, Cannes loses its habitual cool. The rest of the year the city devotes itself to its touristic vocation—as an elegant, cosmopolitan resort in a beautiful setting, with the liveliest pleasure port on the Riviera.

The history of Cannes is linked to the two islands you can see off the coast, the Lérins. On the smaller one, St. Honorat founded a monastery in the 4th century which became a famous shrine for pilgrims. In the 10th century the Count of Antibes gave the Cannes mainland to the Lérins monks. They built ramparts to defend the lands against incursions by Moorish pirates.

By 1788, only four monks remained; the monastery was closed down and Cannes came under French rule. In 1815, Napoleon stopped there after landing at Golfe-Juan. But Cannes gave him such a chilly reception that he had to move on to Grasse.

Like Nice's Promenade des Anglais, the **Croisette** is a magnificent showcase with gleaming hotels lining a flowered boulevard. The golden sand of the beach along the promenade is mainly imported from Fréjus. At one end of the Croisette lies the old port and the new **Palais des Festivals;** at the other, a second port and the Palm Beach Casino. The film festival plus multiple other festivities are held in the grand new Palais, which contains a casino as well.

Just a few blocks behind the Croisette is the **Rue d'Antibes,**

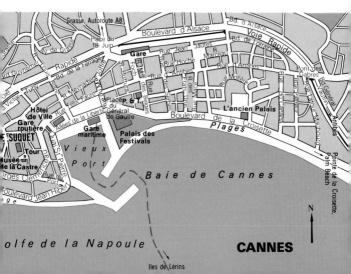

one of the coast's most glamorous shopping streets. For more down-to-earth wares—like tee-shirts, sandals, mouth-watering sausages and pastries—head for Rue Meynadier.

Looking uphill from the old port in the evening, you have a vision of the ramparts of the old town, **Le Suquet,** glowing with orange lights against the dark purple sky. You'll also see the **Tour du Suquet,** a 72-foot-high square watchtower built by the Lérins monks. It was destroyed during the Revolution, but later restored, as a favour to local fishermen who petitioned for a tall, visible navigational point. Now the white stone clock tower is a Cannes trademark.

The centre of the old town is Place de la Castre (from the Latin word for castle), a quiet, pine-shaded square. The 17th century "Gothic" church here, rather dim inside, has several polychrome statues. The **Musée**

**de la Castre** (closed Tuesdays) houses a quaintly eclectic assemblage of everything from an Egyptian mummy's hand to a Japanese warrior's costume and a South Pacific hut pole. The Persian objects are quite good. The donor of all this, a Dutchman named Baron Lycklama, is portrayed in an extraordinary Oriental outfit.

The view over Cannes from Le Suquet is superb. For an even more spectacular panorama, go to the **observatory** at Super-Cannes.

### Iles de Lérins

One of Cannes' most refreshing diversions is an excursion to the islands. Boats leave frequently in the summer: the trip to Sainte-Marguerite takes about 15

*Cannes Film Festival—a field day for cinema fans and fanciers.*

minutes; to Saint-Honorat, 30. In season, they hold sound-and-light shows.

About a mile and a half of wooded hills, a minute "main" street lined with fishermen's houses and a couple of restaurants, **Sainte-Marguerite** is the closer and larger island. It takes its name from St. Honorat's sister who founded her own religious order.

Walk uphill to visit the old **Fort Royal,** built under Cardinal Richelieu, and enjoy a marvellous view of Cannes, Antibes and the hills. The main attraction here is the dank and smelly prison of the "Man in the Iron Mask". There's nothing to see but chains, faded ochre stone and modern graffiti, but the legend is intriguing.

Between 1687 and 1698 a masked prisoner was kept here. Actually his mask was of cloth, not iron, but he wore it constantly and nobody knows for sure who he was or why he was imprisoned. One theory identifies him as an illegitimate brother of Louis XIV; another as the larcenous ex-finance minister Fouquet.

On Sainte-Marguerite you can walk for hours among cool, fragrant woods and a grove of enormous eucalyptus trees, a Riviera staple that was first brought to the coast from Australia in the early 19th century.

The island of **Saint-Honorat,** home of the monks who governed Cannes for nearly eight centuries, is once again a monastery, run by the Cistercian Order. Bright green and gentle with umbrella pines, roses, lavender and the monks' vineyard, it's a peaceful retreat in the off-season. Wandering around you'll come upon several small Romanesque barrel-vaulted chapels.

The most striking construction on Saint-Honorat is the square, battlemented **"château"**—really a fortified dungeon. Built in the

11th century over a Roman cistern, it served as a refuge for the monks during various attacks.

The 19th century monastery is only open for special visits on request. However, you can see the small museum and church, accompanied by a guide. Next door to the museum the monks do a brisk trade in handicrafts, lavender scent and their own liqueur—a redoubtable-looking yellowish liquid.

### Around Cannes

The coast's most glorious oddity, the **Château de la Napoule** (8 km. west of Cannes), hovers in red-rock splendour over a coin-sized beach and harbour. Here, in 1919, American sculptor Henry Clews (scion of a New York banking family) restored the medieval château with towers and battlements, endowing every possible inch with his own work. Wildly imaginative, the sculptures range from a poignant Don Quixote to pudgy grotesques of African inspiration.

The eccentric Clews, who saw himself as a latter-day Quixote and his wife as "the Virgin of La Mancha", filled his home with mottoes, ridiculing the "aberrations" of society.

The museum can be visited by guided tour only, held twice daily at 3 and 4 p.m. except on Tuesdays.

A soft and subtle backdrop of green hills characterizes the countryside between Cannes and Grasse, the *arrière-pays*.

Interesting stops include MOUGINS, a 15th century fortified town (with a few superb restaurants); VALBONNE, with its beautiful arcaded square shaded by big elms and a brightly restored Romanesque church; and PLASCASSIER, a sleepy village on a hill.

# The Esterel

Between Cannes and Saint-Raphaël lies a mass of porphyry rocks worn down and chipped by streams. This is the Esterel, now not much more than 2,000 feet at its highest, though the landscape seems abrupt and impressive. In the spring, the scrub-herb hills are golden with mimosa. The original inland road through the Esterel was the Aurelian Way, built by the Roman emperor in the 3rd century.

These days, most people take the Côte d'Azur motorway between Cannes and Saint-Raphaël, but the coastal route —the **Corniche d'Or** (the Golden Corniche)—is certainly prettier. Reddish porphyry rocks tumble into the dark blue sea making a jigsaw pattern of colours and shapes, tempting you **59** to stop at every outcrop to admire the view.

After LA NAPOULE and then THÉOULE, with its "château" that served as a soap factory in the 18th century, you come to PORT-LA-GALÈRE, a cascade of modern houses on a flowered stony point. The Esterel is full of little resort towns with euphonic names—LE TRAYAS, ANTHÉOR, AGAY. The **Sémaphore du Dramont,** built on the ruins of a watch-tower, offers sweeping views of the coast, and near the road is a marble monument commemorating the American landing here on August 15, 1944.

The best time to see this coast is at sunset looking east, when colours and contrasts are most flamboyant, a surrealist's dream.

### Saint-Raphaël

Focus for the Esterel holiday area, booming Saint-Raphaël is an appealing resort built around a port for pleasure boats.

The town's centre is a palm-lined modern sea-front (the old one was destroyed during the Second World War) with an ornamental fountain and pyramid commemorating Napoleon's debarkation after the 1799 Egyptian victories.

In days gone by, there was a small holiday resort here for Romans based in Fréjus. It stood more or less on the site of the present casino—if you can imagine the clicking roulette tables replaced by luxurious tile baths and fish ponds.

The 12th century Templars' church in the old town is surmounted with a massive watch-tower replacing the right-hand apse.

### Fréjus

Little remains of the busy Roman market town of Fréjus (Forum Julii) founded in 49 B.C. The big harbour, built by Augustus into a great naval base and shipyard, has been completely filled up with silt deposits and replaced by modern Fréjus. A good part of the town was rebuilt after the 1959 catastrophe, when a dam upstream over the River Reyran broke, killing over 400 people.

Most impressive of the Roman vestiges is the **arena,** a restored grey-green construction which could seat 10,000 spectators—nearly as large as the arenas of Arles and Nîmes. It's closed on Tuesdays. During the season, bullfights are held here. Other Roman ruins include a theatre and big reddish arches of the aqueduct that brought water in from the River Siagnole.

*Stopping point on the Esterel: splendid views at every turn.*

Nearly razed by Saracens in the 10th century, Fréjus was revived in 990 by Bishop Riculphe, who established a fortified **episcopal city** here with a cathedral, baptistery, cloister and bishop's palace. Apply to a side entrance for a guided tour to see the carved Renaissance doors, the baptistery and the cloisters.

One of the oldest religious buildings in France (late 4th to early 5th century), the octagonal **baptistery** is punctuated by handsome black granite columns with Corinthian capitals (from the ancient Fréjus forum). The terra-cotta baptismal bowl, the original, was unearthed in the course of archaeological research.

In the **cloister,** a double-deckered arcade surrounds a garden

*A provincial Colosseum—the Roman arena at Fréjus held 10,000 people.*

of roses and cypress trees. The ceiling of the upstairs arcade is decorated with some amusing 14th century creatures—imaginative scenes from the Apocalypse. An archaeological museum adjoining the cloister has Gallo-Roman remains.

The 10th to 12th century **cathedral,** with its "broken cradle" vaulting, exemplifies the early Gothic style of the region. It was built on the site of a Roman temple dedicated to Jupiter.

# Côte des Maures

On the way to Saint-Tropez, you'll pass through the attractive little town of SAINTE-MAXIME, with a casino, a minute beach and a wide promenade. In the summer it's packed with people who would love to be in Saint-Tropez but can't find a hotel room there.

### Saint-Tropez

It barely manages to keep up with its glamorous reputation: celebrity escapades, the beauty of its little port, cafés filled with fashionable people, chic boutiques and casual nudity on nearby beaches.

Brigitte Bardot avoids the crowds now, but other stars still come out at night to haunt the "in" cafés and discotheques. In Saint-Tropez more than any other place on the Riviera you feel an unspoken desire to wear the right tee-shirt, be seen with the right people, show up in certain places at certain times of day or night. The atmosphere is enlivened by clusters of motorcycles roaring by, as well as haughty mannequins and golden boys with big dogs. In winter it reverts back to an easy-going fishing town.

Saint-Tropez weathers its own snobbery while cultivating its legends. The name comes from a Roman Christian, Torpes (an officer of the capricious Nero), who was martyred in Pisa in A.D. 68. The headless body, put adrift in a small boat with a dog and a cock, came ashore in the Var region. In the local church you can see a tableau of the body drifting along with its animal companion, as well as a wide-eyed sculpture of the saint himself, neatly mustachioed, surrounded with a lacy halo, his chest covered with heart-shaped medals.

The town was battered several times by the Saracens, and more recently by the German occupation and invasions of World War II. But the gallant little fishing village always managed to come back; in 1637 it routed a fleet of invading Spanish ships and still **63**

celebrates the victory in May with the Bravade, a fête that also honours St. Tropez himself. The natives get out their muskets, don 17th and 18th century costumes and happily fire blanks all over the place in noisy parades with fife, drums, fireworks and cannon shots from the old fort. (There is a similar but less important festival in mid-June.)

Saint-Tropez was first "discovered" by the French writer **64** Guy de Maupassant; it became very fashionable in the twenties, when it was visited and painted by Dunoyer de Segonzac, Dufy, Bonnard, and Signac; Colette wrote reams in her villa here, La Treille Muscate.

After World War II, the town managed to put itself together again in its former style, wisely rejecting plans for modern urban development.

You can't miss the **port** with its restless crowds, shiny yachts and pastel houses with red tile

*Market day—gossip and good humour are the order of the day .*

roofs, most of them rebuilt in the old fishermen's style. Nearby the plane-tree-shaded **Place des Lices** is crowded with local colour: a food market takes over several mornings a week, and *pétanque* (bowls) games are the centre of interest in the late afternoon.

The **Musée de l'Annonciade,** a former chapel situated on the west side of the port, houses an excellent collection of Impressionist and Post-Impressionist works. Many of the artists lived in and loved Saint-Tropez. You can view paintings by Signac, Van Dongen, Dufy, Bonnard and others in rooms lit by refracted Saint-Tropez sunshine. Outside, the quay space is crowded with contemporary artists, trying their best to sell their work, which can only be called "wares" compared **65** to the paintings contained in the Annonciade.

A short walk behind the Quai Jean-Jaurès will take you to the old town—through an arcade by La Ponche (the old fishing port), past narrow old buildings now housing expensive hotels and boutiques, to the 17th century **Citadel** on top of the hill.

*Saint-Tropez: sun and games at Tahiti beach.*

The moat, surrounded with greenery, is living quarters for preening peacocks, a few duck and deer. The Musée de la Marine here contains souvenirs of a locally born hero, Admiral de Suffren (who took his fleet on an odyssey around the Cape of Good Hope in 1781), model ships and diving equipment.

Saint-Tropez is noted for its beaches. Nearby ones like the Plage des Graniers and the Bouillabaisse are popular with

local people on weekends, but holiday visitors look down their noses at them. They drive out to Les Salins or the vast sandy crescent (6 miles long) that stretches in front of green vineyards from Tahiti beach via Pampelonne to Cap Camarat.

Smooth-sanded and bordering a clear aquamarine sea, the beaches are fully equipped in summer with all manner of huts and shacks to furnish mattresses, umbrellas and sustenance to sunbathers. Part of the beach is traditionally given over to nudists —of all shapes; other areas are more or less discreet and more or less chic; each has its own style. Every summer the beautiful people gravitate to the bar-restaurant-beach of the moment.

## More Ports and Hill Towns

Saint-Tropez is surrounded by delightful spots to visit when you've had enough of the beach scene.

A short trip will take you to GASSIN and RAMATUELLE— towns with panoramic views and pleasant restaurants—and the ruins of MOULINS DE PAILLAS. They provide an introduction to the **Maures** mountains, the oldest geological mass of Provence: worn-down cristalline hills, green and covered with pines and scrub trees.

Going north into the Maures over a long road full of hairpin bends, through thick forests of chestnut and cork, you come to LA GARDE-FREINET. At 1,329 feet, the town is considerably cooler than the coast. It has a natural, unspoilt charm that attracts crowd-weary Parisians. It also makes a living off the land— corks and chestnuts.

The ruins of an old fortress evoke the last stand of the marauding Saracens. For several **67**

centuries these pirates of Arab origin managed to hold out here as they pillaged the towns below—until they were thrown out in 973.

If you're pressed for time, forget La Garde-Freinet but stop at GRIMAUD—best in the late afternoon, when you can look out to sea through Provençal lotus trees and enjoy a drink in a café. Grimaud was the fiefdom of Gibalin (Ghibellin) de Grimaldi.

The fortress ruins stand up in piles of stony remnants against a grassy hill. A sign warns you not to poke around here because of the danger of falling rocks, but you can take a look at the simple, barrel-vaulted 11th century Templars' church (this is a restored version) and the arcaded charterhouse.

PORT-GRIMAUD, 6.5 kilometres downhill on the bay of Saint-Tropez, is the French modern version of Venice. Designed by François Spoerry and opened in 1964, it is a series of artificial canals built on marshland, lined with pleasant little houses and terraces painted in the same colours as Saint-Tropez.

For most French people, the Riviera stops at Saint-Tropez (some even say Saint-Raphaël),

*Inland, the place to find an old*
**68** *fortress and fragrant fresh herbs.*

but the coast does go on. Not always the prettiest stretch, it is spoiled in parts by 20th century concrete construction.

Still reasonably pleasant, however, are a string of small resort towns—LA CROIX-VALMER, CAVALAIRE, PRAMOUSQUIER and RAYOL—in flowered settings under the Maures hills.

LE LAVANDOU, originally a colourful spot, has suffered from urbanism, though it's still quite popular. The town has a pretty beachside promenade and is a good starting-point for excursions. From here, go uphill and you'll come to BORMES-LES-MIMOSAS, a lovely retreat that lives up to its name—blooming not only with mimosa, but also oleander, roses, geraniums and bougainvillea.

**Hyères** is the "granny" of Mediterranean resorts. The French were coming to this picturesque old city, attracted by its extremely mild climate, as early as the 18th century, even before the English started to winter in Nice. Queen Victoria sometimes chose to stay here on her visits to the Riviera. On the Place de la République, you'll see a 13th century **church** where St. Louis, King of France, prayed after his return from a crusade in 1254; Hyères was the landing port for returning crusaders, though they disembarked at what is now the middle of town. Today modern boulevards run right over the old harbour.

Hyères is a busy city featuring an uphill market street, Rue Massillon (go in the morning when it's in full swing), the old town, an ancient Templars' building and the Eglise Saint-Paul (a Gothic church renovated in the 16th century). From the square you have a panoramic view.

## Iles d'Hyères

Also known as the Iles d'Or ("golden islands") because of their shiny, mica-shot rocks—sometimes mistaken for gold—they are three: Levant, Port-Cros and Porquerolles. You can easily visit them by taking a ferry across from Hyères and Le Lavandou or even from Toulon or Cavalaire.

The long, rocky **Ile du Levant** is France's nudist capital, where one of the first nudist colonies

*Instead of taking a noon siesta, this fisherman repairs his nets.*

was established in the early 1930s. You can keep your trousers on, but refrain from obvious gawking and photography: the *naturistes* don't like to be treated as curiosities. The eastern half of the island is seriously off-limits—there is a naval base here.

71

Next to the Levant lies **Ile de Port-Cros,** covered with steep myrtle- and heather-decked hills and an abundance of bird life. This protected national park boasts resident flamingoes, turtle-doves, cormorants and puffins, plus rare flowers, orchids, and mushrooms when it's the season (boletus and chanterelles).

The largest island, **Porquerolles** (5 miles long, 2 miles wide), is another enchanting setting, with lovely sandy beaches along its north shore (where the boat lands), vineyards and pinewoods in its interior, and a southern shoreline of steep, rocky cliffs. There are some excellent small beaches and coves for bathing on these islands, but you'll probably not be alone in the high season.

# From Toulon to Marseilles

## Toulon
*Pop. 172,000*

Military buffs love Toulon, France's big naval port, which reeks of maritime history. Its picturesque seafront was devastated during World War II, but even now with its modern concrete seaport blocks, it retains a certain dignity.

Toulon was pushed into prominence in the 17th century by Cardinal Richelieu, who saw the potential of a great natural harbour. Under Louis XIV, the military engineer Vauban was commissioned to fortify and enlarge the facilities.

World War II was a tragedy for the naval centre. Nearly the

MARSEILLES–TOULON

whole French fleet was scuttled on November 27, 1942, to keep it from falling into German hands. Two years later the port was battered by Allied troops, and then the Germans blew up their installations before leaving, wreaking still more havoc. But with modern reconstruction, Toulon has regained its former importance.

Broad, busy Boulevard de Strasbourg (off Place de la Liberté) runs through the heart of Toulon, slicing the city in half. On the north is the newer, more residential area; to the south, the remains of the **old town.** Head in this direction for Place Puget, a charming Provençal square (just behind the Municipal Theatre) with a dolphin fountain and lots of greenery. Downhill is the narrow market street, Rue d'Alger, a favourite for evening strolling.

Off to the left, the cathedral, **Sainte-Marie-Majeure** (also known as Sainte-Marie de la Seds), has a handsome baroque façade and belfry (18th century). Another block east is the Cours Lafayette, one of the most animated indoor-outdoor market streets in Europe, where you can buy everything from flowers to leather souvenirs. History enthusiasts can visit the nearby Musée Historique du Vieux-Toulon.

The **port** is a particularly lively part of town. Look out for the magnificently muscled caryatids (Atlantes de Puget, dating from the 17th century) on the façade of the **Mairie d'Honneur** on the Quai Stalingrad; they represent Strength and Weariness. They look as if they were shouldering the world—and they're about all that's left of the old port. The **Musée Naval** (closed Tuesdays in low season) contains some impressive boat models.

Across from the public garden in the west central part of town are the **Musée d'Art** and **Muséum d'Histoire Naturelle** (both closed on bank holidays). The former has a collection of contemporary art and paintings from the Provençal school (17th to 20th century).

**Mont Faron** (1,778 feet) commands a grandiose view of Toulon, the surrounding mountains and the coast. You can get there by car via a steep, sinuous route or take a *téléphérique* from the Faron Corniche (Gare Inférieure, Bd. Amiral-Vence). At the top you'll find a wooded park, picnic areas, children's play areas, restaurants and a zoo. Close by is the Tour Beaumont, a war museum containing information about the Liberation.

Inland excursions from Toulon include **Le Gros Cerveau** mountain for a magnificent panorama, the rugged **Gorges d'Ollioules,** the 16th century castle remnants of **Evenos** and another look-out 73 point at **Mont Caume.** If you have time to venture further north, the **Massif de la Sainte-Baume** offers the irregular hilly landscape typical of Provence, a venerable forest and a stunning view from **Saint-Pilon.**

### Côte des Calanques

The limestone coastline between Toulon and Marseilles is riddled with deep, uneven inlets *(calanques)*. This stretch, backed by the green scrub of the *maquis,* has inevitably spawned holiday developments. But you can still find attractive natural sites.

Well-sheltered SANARY, with sandy beaches and an old port, is the first town you come to on the Baies du Soleil (sunny bays). **Bandol** takes honours as the area's leading resort. It has a mild climate and long beach lined with housing developments. It is known for its vineyards which produce good red and white wine.

You can make a pleasant side trip to the privately owned island of **Bendor.** This site boasts a reproduction of a Provençal village and museums devoted to the sea and to wine.

One of the world's largest shipyards, LA CIOTAT has managed to retain a small bit of its original charm. Against the background of towering cranes and steel hulls of the busy modern shipyard, the old fishing port holds out doggedly—typically Provençal with nets, small boats and colourful houses.

The port of **Cassis** may seem familiar—paintings of it by artists like Vlaminck, Matisse and Dufy hang in museums all over the world. Today you'll see the same gaily-coloured stucco houses and crisp little triangular sails bobbing on the clear blue

*Limestone cliffs of Calanques drop off abruptly into the sea.*

water. Hovering in the background are the rocks of La Gardiole and the tree-covered Cap Canaille, at 1,400 ft the highest cliff in all of Continental Europe.

Cassis is mainly known for its incomparable shellfish, its *bouillabaisse* (fish soup) and its white wine, appreciated all over the

south (but not to be confused with the *cassis,* blackcurrant, syrup or liqueur).

From Cassis you'll probably want to visit some *calanques,* best done in a rented boat or on a tour. The most spectacular of them all is **d'En Vau**—a mini-fjord with limpid blue-green water fingering through the rocky cliffs to a minute crescent of a white beach.

### Marseilles
Though not really part of the French Riviera, this great city (*Marseille* to the French) merits a visit for many reasons. France's largest port, its second largest metropolis and its oldest, Marseilles has played a major role in the country's history.

It offers excellent shopping, an international atmosphere, big industry, interesting museums and very good food: some of the best *bouillabaisse* on the coast is to be found here, particularly around the Old Port and on the Corniche (Vallon des Auffres).

Be sure to wander around the old port, first used by the Phoceans in 600 B.C., and to see the impressive facilities of the modern port. You can also tour it by boat.

*Maritime parking lot in Marseilles for small craft and fishing boats.*

# What to Do

## Museums
The French Riviera is studded with excellent museums (some described more fully under town headings). Most are open mornings 9 or 10 a.m. to noon, and afternoons 2 to 6 p.m. (winter), 3 to 7 p.m. (summer).

### Antibes
All the museums are closed Tuesdays and in November.
*Musée Grimaldi-Picasso,* Place du Château, prodigious Picasso collection (see p. 44).
*Musée Archéologique,* Bastion Saint-André, local antiquities.
*Musée Naval et Napoléonien,* Eden-Roc Cap d'Antibes, Napoleonic souvenirs.

### Beaulieu
*Villa Kérylos,* 2.30 to 6.30 p.m. July/August, 2 to 6 p.m. the rest of the year, closed Monday, November and the first week of December (see pp. 31–32).

### Biot
*Musée National Fernand Léger,* impressive one-man retrospective; closed Tuesdays (see p. 47).

### Cagnes-sur-Mer
*Château-Musée,* modern art works and olive museum; closed

Tuesdays and from October 15 to November 15 (see pp. 47–48).

**Cannes**
*Musée de la Castre,* Le Suquet, eclectic collection; closed on Tuesday.

**Grasse**
*Musée d'Art et d'Histoire de Provence,* closed Monday and Tuesday.
*Musée Fragonard,* open daily.

**La Napoule**
*Château* (Henry Clews Foundation), impressive sculptures in a stylish setting; guided tours daily at 3 p.m. and 4 p.m. Closed Tuesday.

**Monaco**
*Musée National,* open every day except public holidays; *Palais du Prince,* open all day from June 1 to October 31; *Musée Océanographique,* open every day (see pp. 38, 40, 41–42).

**Nice**
*Musée Palais Masséna,* 35, Promenade des Anglais, an old mansion with a good collection of Empire furnishings, historical exhibits, paintings from the 15th to 16th century Nice school, Impressionist paintings. Open from 10 a.m. to noon, 2 to 5 p.m., 3 to 6 p.m. June to September, closed Monday.

*Musée des Beaux-Arts Jules-Chéret,* 33, avenue des Baumettes, outstanding Impressionist paintings and lovely pastels by Chéret, works by Gustav-Adolf Mossa, a symbolist whose eerie, intricate dream-fantasies deserve to be better known. Open 10 a.m. to noon, 2 to 5 p.m., 2 to 6 p.m. June to September, closed Monday.

*Palais Lascaris,* 15, rue Droite, baroque palace in the heart of old Nice (see pp. 22–23). Open 9 a.m. to noon, 2.30 to 6 p.m., closed Monday and November.

*Musée du Vieux-Logis,* 59, avenue Saint-Barthélemy, historical collection featuring Gothic statuary, religious paintings and stained glass. Open 3 to 5 p.m., Wednesday, Thursday and Saturday only.

*Musée de Malacologie,* 3, cours Saleya, seashells galore. Open 10.30 a.m. to 1 p.m., 2 to 6.30 p.m., closed Sunday and Monday.

*Musée de Terra Amata,* 25, boulevard Carnot, an engaging view of prehistoric man around Nice. Open 9 a.m. to noon, 2 to 6 p.m., closed Monday and first two weeks of September.

*Musée Matisse et d'Archéologie,* 164, avenue des Arènes, Cimiez (see p. 26–27). Open 10 a.m. to noon, 2 to 6 p.m., closed Monday and first two weeks of September.

*Monumental sculpture by Léger stands near his museum in Biot.*

*Musée Chagall,* avenue du Docteur-Ménard, biblical themes displayed in a modern setting. Open 10 a.m. to 12.30 p.m., 2 to 5.30 p.m., 10 a.m. to 7 p.m. July to September, closed Tuesday.

*Musée International d'Art Naïf,* Château Sainte-Hélène, Avenue Val Marie; entrance free. Open 10 a.m. to noon, 2 to 6 p.m., 2 to 5 p.m. October to April, closed Thursday.

*Musée d'Art Moderne et d'Art Contemporain,* Promenade des Anglais. An important collection of European contemporary art. Open 11 a.m. to 8 p.m. (10 p.m. on Friday), closed Thursday.

### Saint-Jean-Cap-Ferrat

*Fondation Ephrussi de Rothschild,* "Belle Epoque" dwelling and gardens. Open 10 a.m. to noon, 2 to 6 p.m., 2 to 7 p.m. July to August, closed Sunday morning, Monday and November (see p. 30).

**Saint-Tropez**
*Musée de l'Annonciade,* a sunny display of 20th century paintings on the old port; closed Tuesday, November (see p. 65).

*Brilliant bouquet crowns every important festival on the Riviera.*

**Saint-Paul-de-Vence**
*Fondation Maeght,* one of the world's great modern art museums; open every day (see p. 49).

**Vence**
*La Chapelle du Rosaire,* the famous Matisse chapel; open Tuesday and Thursday 10 to 11.30 a.m. and 2.30 to 5.30 p.m. (more frequently from July to September), closed public holidays and November 1 to mid-December (see p. 51).

## Festivals and Other Events

The Riviera's calendar is filled with festivals and religious pageants (especially around Lent, Easter and Christmas), plus major artistic and sporting events. Here are just a few of the outstanding ones:

**January**
*Monte Carlo.* Automobile Rally.
*Cannes.* MIDEM, international recording and music-publishing fair.

**February**
*Nice.* The Carnival fills the streets with floats, girls and gaiety in the two weeks preceding Shrove Tuesday.
*Cannes.* The mimosa festival celebrates nature.
*Menton.* During the Lemon Festival the town takes on a golden glow with citrus mosaics everywhere and parades.

**March**
*Nice.* Battle of Flowers, Provençal dancing (Easter).

**April**
*Monte Carlo.* Tennis Championships.

**May**
*Cannes.* The International Film Festival stirs frenzy for a few weeks.
*Saint-Tropez.* The Bravade (see p. 64), is a costumed, noisy event commemorating local victories, May 16-18.
*Monaco.* The Grand Prix motor race.
*Grasse.* International Rose Exhibition.

**June**
*Antibes.* Festival of St. Peter, sailors' religious celebration (last Sunday in June).
*Nice.* Festival of Sacred Music.
*Saint-Tropez.* Second Bravade (June 15).

**July**
July 14, Bastille Day and National Day. Celebrations with fireworks in all towns and villages.
*Antibes/Juan-les-Pins.* Jazz Festival.
*Monaco.* Firework Festival.
*Nice (Cimiez).* Jazz Festival.

**August**
*Menton.* International Chamber Music Festival.
*Roquebrune.* Passion procession through old town (August 5).

**October**
*Cannes.* VIDCOM, international video fair.

# For Children

Besides the myriad of sporting activities, there's lots to amuse children around the Riviera. Monaco, Cap Ferrat (don't miss the afternoon monkey show), Fréjus and Toulon all have zoos.

The Monaco Oceanographic Museum has an excellent aquarium, while Marineland between Antibes and Biot offers penguins, seals and an afternoon dolphin show. In Marseilles there is the Aquarium du Prado. More unusual is O.K. Corral, a Western theme park on the RN8 Cuges-les-Pins, east of Aubagne.

Monaco's Musée National features beautifully dressed dolls and mechanical puppets that perform wind-up tricks. The wax museum in Monaco is also a favourite with children.

# Shopping

Most shops are open from 8 or 9 a.m. to noon and from 2 to 7 p.m., Tuesday to Saturday (many stores close on Monday); large department stores do not close for lunch. Otherwise hours can be casual. In the summer, small shops often close for longer periods in the middle of the day, but stay open later in the evening for the tourist trade. They may also open on Sundays.

### Best Buys
The coast is a mouth-watering bazaar, and will delight even the most jaded shopper. You can find the best of everything French—jewellery, couturier clothing, silverware, crystal and

even furs. In Nice (Rue de France), Cannes (Rue d'Antibes) and Monte Carlo (around the casino), the shopping areas are on a par with Paris.

*What to buy? Wooden antiques or an abstract print made yesterday.*

In the mini-luxury category, good buys include silk scarves, perfumes, liqueurs and even scented soaps. Sportswear is highly recommended, especially for women. The latest thing is always displayed in little boutiques and aggressively brushes your nose on the quayside at

Saint-Tropez, where you can hardly go through the yards of tee-shirts without purchasing something.

## Arts and Crafts

You'll see some beautiful pottery, glazed stoneware and ceramic work, particularly around Vallauris, Saint-Paul-de-

*Olives galore on market day in Place des Lices, Saint-Tropez.*

Vence and Biot. Anything from simple ashtrays to entire dinner sets—plain, flowery, contemporary abstract, even some original Picasso designs. The heavy, bubbled Biot glasswork in subtle colours fits well in a country-home setting.

Semi-precious stones, often set in jewellery, are abundant in shop windows. You'll frequently see olive-wood tables, stools, salad sets and bracelets—especially in the towns near Cannes.

The famous, attractively flowered Provençal cotton is ubiquitous; you can purchase it in bolts or made up into cushions, carry-all bags, small shoulder bags, skirts or quilts.

## Antiques and Art

You'll find old Provençal tables and commodes, brass clocks and candlesticks, copper cooking utensils, rare and common china patterns and plenty of "kitsch".

If you're looking for art works, you'll find endless possibilities at all prices. There are hundreds of galleries selling paintings and sculptures by famous and local names: around the ports, painters turn out their rendition of the scene and sell at whatever price they can get.

## Souvenirs

Looking for a picture of the port of Cannes on a fringed satin flag, an ash-tray with the local château on it? Almost anything decorated with portraits of the royal family of Monaco? Your wishes will be easily gratified.

For philatelists, there are the beautifully printed Monaco stamps; for children, favourites like sea-shell jewellery and traditionally costumed dolls.

## Shopping Tips

If you have the time, compare prices in different shops before buying. You can always try to bargain at stands or small shops, but it rarely works, especially when a price tag is attached. Sometimes, though, you will receive a special discount with a big purchase.

If you're returning home to a non-Common Market country, ask about the possibility of a refund of the value-added tax (TVA) on larger purchases. You must fill out a form, give a copy to the customs when leaving France and later receive your refund at home. (Beware, however, of bank clearance charges on foreign cheques.)

Shops with "duty-free" signs in the windows often give the TVA refund even on small purchases. The international airport is a good place to purchase duty-free items, especially liquor and perfumes.

# Sports and Games

The Riviera's climate makes it ideal for outdoor sports, and facilities are generally first-rate.

## Swimming

In the official classification of beaches by cleanliness, the Côte d'Azur does well; of its 143 beaches, only 6 are "C"-grade (usable), all the others being

"A"- or "B"-grade (impeccable or virtually pollution-free).

Beach concessionaires charge entry and/or changing-room fees at many bathing areas. You can also indulge yourself a little and rent a mattress (practically indispensable on some of the stony beaches). But of course, there are also free—if not always spic and span—public beaches. The other trick is a fee for parking. If you prefer a pool, there are many of them charging a small fee for entry.

### Water-skiing
*Ski nautique* can be found at all the larger beaches (Nice, Cannes, Antibes and so on). Real daredevils go for kite-skiing.

### Windsurfing
Windsurfing is a well-established sport along the coast and boards *(planche à voile)* can be hired in all the major resorts. If you are new to the sport, courses are available.

### Scuba Diving, Snorkelling
There are diving centres at Antibes, Cagnes, Cannes, Monte

*The exuberance of scuba divers contrasts with the quiet joys of angling in a mountain stream.*

Carlo and Nice. Equipment may be hired and instruction arranged at centres in these localities.

## Fishing

The piscine population of the Mediterranean is suffering from over-fishing and pollution. But you can spend a few pleasant hours with baited hook around the coast or take a day-tour on a fishing boat. Real sportsmen like to angle for trout in the mountain streams. Inquire about licence regulations.

## Boating and Sailing

The coast is lined with first-class yacht facilities. If you require the best of everything but haven't brought your own boat, you can hire a 30-metre vessel with a ten-man crew and enjoy "the life of Riley". Smaller boats, of course, are also available for those with

*Anyone can take a crack at it.*

more modest requirements and tighter budgets.

For an idea of what it might cost to hire a boat, see p. 104. Cannes and Antibes are the biggest rental centres.

## Tennis
You find tennis courts almost everywhere along the coast. The proper attire and payment of an hourly court fee will admit you to most clubs. In summer you may have to book a day ahead.

## Golf
The best in France—with scenic 18-hole courses at Mougins, Biot, Mandelieu-La Napoule, Valbonne (all clustered around Cannes), Monte Carlo (Mont-Agel), and a few 9-hole courses. You can hire clubs, though it's advisable to bring your own shoes and golf balls, as these are expensive in France.

## Horse-riding
There are lots of possibilities for riding, often "ranch" style in the country behind the coast.

## Skiing
About two hours from the coast are 11 winter sports areas, some very well developed. Best-known are Isola 2000 (where they teach the new graduated short-ski method), Auron and Valberg.

## Other Activities
You can play the local *pétanque* (or *boules*) if the natives will initiate you to this bowling game; but every sport is available somewhere—from regular bowling, judo and archery to table tennis. If you're feeling fit, hire a bicycle and pedal around the hills alongside the fanatics practising for semi- or professional races. The Riviera's modern racecourse is at Cros-de-Cagnes, near the Nice airport.

# Nightlife

The Riviera is a night-crawler's dream. From the very first seaside aperitif to well after midnight or even till dawn, nocturnal activity is hectic. Some people can hardly drag themselves to the beach the next day. Possibilities range from "pub" crawling around some of the dock areas (Nice, Toulon) to the most elegant balls in the world, particularly at Monte Carlo.

## Cultural Activities
On the dignified side, the coast offers the best in music and ballet. Monte Carlo's opera house features brilliant opera, concerts, ballet and theatre the year round; summer concerts in the palace courtyard are particularly popu-

lar (try to book in advance). Ticket prices for concerts and opera vary considerably.

Menton has a famous music festival in August; Nice, its own opera house with good theatre in the winter; Toulon, a municipal theatre that also presents concerts and ballet; Marseilles an opera and several theatres including the famous La Criée. The latest films are shown in French or dubbed in French.

### Nightclubs and Discotheques

For slick floorshows or elegant dining and dancing, go to Nice, Monte Carlo or Cannes. As you **90** would expect, the discotheque

*Well-heeled visitors enjoy sumptuous show at Monte Carlo casino.*

scene is frenetic but you can get in almost anywhere.

Monte Carlo has the most elegant discos, Saint-Tropez the most attractive clientele, and in between you'll find everything, with a particularly rowdy ambiance at Juan-les-Pins in summer. Dine late, because discos don't start to warm up till 11 p.m.

### Casinos

The tense atmosphere may not be apparent in the streets, but for some here gambling is a way of life. Monte Carlo started the ball rolling in 1860, and the other towns joined the profitable bandwagon 50 years later. Now at least 20 casinos operate between Menton and Sainte-Maxime.

Every game goes—from the non-stop slot machines to baccarat. The casinos usually open after 3 p.m. (hours vary) and stay open till the last discouraged customer quits, but for early birds, Monte Carlo's main casino opens at 10 a.m. Entry prices vary from place to place, but entrance to Monte Carlo casino is free. Most establishments ask to see your passport.

# Wining and Dining

Wandering through the streets of a southern French town, you can often guess what's cooking for dinner. Marvellous aromas—of fresh rosemary or thyme, all-pervading garlic, fragrant olive oil, the smoky smell of charcoal-broiled meat or fish—waft through the air. Add to that images of the plump and juicy tomatoes, glistening green and red peppers, dark purple aubergines, silvery sardines, all fresh from the market-place, and you'll be ready to sit down to eat.

French cooking reaches great peaks in Provence*. Some of the country's best restaurants here offer exquisite (and expensive) food in incomparable settings. But food can also be deliciously simple with robust flavours. When you see *à la provençale* on a menu, you can be fairly sure garlic, tomato and herbs are part of the recipe. And don't shy away from garlic and onions: they're eminently appropriate in this climate.

## Soup and Salad

*Pistou* is practically a whole meal—a thick vegetable soup made with beans, onions or leeks, fresh herbs, especially basil, and usually garlic, topped with freshly grated cheese.

*Soupe de poisson* can also fill you up for hours. Made with available fish leftovers, tomato, saffron, garlic and onions, it's served with generous garnishings of toast rounds, grated cheese and *rouille,* a hot tomato-garlic-flavoured mayonnaise. *Bourride* is thicker and richer, with lots of fish ground up in it.

Speaking of garlic, try a bracing *aïoli* (when you don't have any important social engagements). You dip boiled fish,

---

*For a comprehensive glossary of French culinary terms and how to order wine, ask your bookshop for the Berlitz EUROPEAN MENU READER.

> **Bouillabaisse**
>
> It's only fish stew, but the mystique surrounding it is substantial enough to fill a Proustian novel. Every chef has his own idea: some say it's heresy to include spiny lobster and that mussels are only for Parisians. Marseilles chefs are appalled by their Toulon confreres' addition of potatoes.
>
> The important thing is really the fresh local seafood—with fascinating names like *rascasse, baudroie, chapon* and *Saint-Pierre*. These can be translated but mean next to nothing away from the Mediterranean. The fish are served in their own broth highly flavoured with wine, cayenne and saffron, and accompanied by crunchy croutons and garlicky red-hot *rouille*.

potatoes, green beans and so on in the heavily perfumed mayonnaise.

The renowned *salade niçoise* can be a treat. Essential ingredients include tomato, anchovies, radishes, green peppers, olives, sometimes cucumbers and artichoke hearts, well doused in a vinaigrette dressing. Tuna, celery, green beans, hard-boiled egg quarters and a few lettuce leaves (the latter anathema to the purists) complete the picture.

Endless mixed salads are offered, many with ham and cheese or seafood. *Salade antiboise* usually combines cooked diced fish and anchovy fillets with green peppers, beetroot, rice and capers with vinaigrette dressing. *Crudités,* a raw vegetable salad, makes a nice light first course.

### Fish

On the Riviera, the aristocrat of fish is the *loup de mer* (sea bass),

best prepared with fennel, flamed. *Daurade,* a tender white fish (gilt-head or sea bream), costs less; it's usually grilled or baked with onion, tomato and lemon juice and a dash of wine, occasionally with garlic and a *pastis* (anis) flavouring. *Rouget* (red mullet) may be served grilled or *en papillotte* (baked in foil with lemon wedges).

The grilled *scampi* (prawns) you'll see on menus everywhere can be good, but they're invariably imported and frozen. *Langouste,* or spiny lobster, costs a king's ransom. It's eaten cold with mayonnaise or hot in a tomato-and-cognac-flavoured sauce *(à l'américaine).*

Mussels *(moules)* are popular *à la marinière* (in white wine), in soup or with savoury stuffings. A lowly but tempting gourmandise

*Mougins—one of the places to find the best in French cuisine.*

is *friture de mer*, crisp-fried small fish to be eaten like chips.

## Meat and Poultry

Steak turns up in various fashions; the good cuts (*entrecôte, côte de bœuf, faux-filet, filet*) are as tasty charcoal-broiled with fresh herbs as with sauces. *Bleu* means almost raw; *saignant*, rare; *à point*, medium done.

Lamb is succulent in the spring; you'll often see *gigot d'agneau* or *côtes d'agneau gril-*lées aux herbes* (leg of lamb or grilled chops with herbs), which the French serve medium rare. *Brochettes*, or skewered kebabs, can be delicious, though the quality depends on the meat chosen by the chef.

*Daube de bœuf* is a traditional beef stew particularly good in Nice. With its aromatic brown,

*Relaxed aperitif hour in Menton on the lively Place aux Herbes.*

wine-flavoured mushroom sauce, accompanied by freshly made noodles *(pâtes fraîches)*, it can be memorable. *Estouffade,* a variation on the theme, adds black olives to the sauce.

Veal dishes are often of Italian inspiration, as in breaded-fried *escalopes milanaises* (scaloppini). But *alouettes sans têtes* are not "headless larks" as the translation would imply: they're small rolled veal cutlets with stuffing (veal birds).

Even tripe-haters are converted by the Niçois version of this dish *(tripes niçoises):* a superb concoction simmered in olive oil, white wine, tomato, onion, garlic and herbs. *Pieds et paquets,* a Marseilles speciality, consists of stuffed tripe and sheeps' trotters cooked with bacon, onion, carrot rounds, white wine, garlic and sometimes tomato.

Chickens are frequently spit-roasted with herbs *(poulet rôti aux herbes); poulet niçoise* is a local fricassee made with white wine, stock, herbs, tomatoes and black olives. Rabbit *(lapin)* can be quite tender, like chicken, and might be served in a mustard sauce or *à la provençale.*

In season (autumn/winter), the menu may list partridge *(perdreau),* pigeon or quail *(caille)* often served with a grape sauce *(aux raisins),* or boar *(marcassin* or *sanglier).*

## Pasta and Vegetables

The Italian influence is strong around Menton and Nice, becoming less so as you go west. You'll often find superb pasta—ravioli, cannelloni, fettuccine, lasagne—rivalling Italy's best.

But the glory of southern France is its fresh vegetables. *Ratatouille*—the celebrated vegetable stew made with tomatoes, onions, aubergine (eggplant), marrow (zucchini) and green peppers—practically stands as a meal in itself, either hot or cold. You'll find stuffed aubergines, marrow and tomatoes well seasoned with local herbs.

Asparagus *(asperges)* are superb served warm with melted butter or hollandaise sauce or cold with *vinaigrette.* Artichokes receive the same treatment or may appear with meat or herb stuffings.

## Cheese and Dessert

In the south you can usually eat classics from the 300-odd varieties of French cheese. But don't miss out on the regionally made goat or sheeps'-milk cheeses *(fromages de chèvre, de brebis).* A few good names: *tomme de Sospel, tomme de chèvre de montagne, brousse de la Vésubie, cabécou, poivre d'âne.*

For dessert, nothing can rival the local fruits in season. Savour the fat, dark-red strawberries **95**

(April–Oct.) dipped in *crème fraîche* (a slightly acid double cream). Melons of all kinds (from Cavaillon, near Aix, they're renowned) taste sweeter than usual. Figs and peaches are equally good. Ices are refreshing, especially the fruit *sorbets*. You can satisfy a sweet tooth with all kinds of fruit tarts and local pastries: *ganses* (small fried cakes topped with sugar), *pignons* (buttery *croissants* with pine-nuts) and the famed *tarte tropézienne* of Saint-Tropez—a rich yellow cake with custard filling and coarse-sugar topping.

## Quick Snacks

Cafés serve hearty sandwiches on long chunks of French bread (pâté, ham or cheese). Thin-sliced bread *(pain de mie)* is used for the delicious *croque-monsieur* (toasted ham-and-cheese sandwich). Omelettes are always reliable fare.

*Tian* is a local term vaguely covering warm or cold stuffed pastry or omelettes sold by street vendors and in some restaurants. The filling is usually an egg-custard, green vegetable mixture. *Tourtes* are pastry turnovers with similar vegetable stuffings.

Another popular local item (great at the beach) is *pan bagnat*—essentially a huge round sandwich filled with tomatoes, hard-boiled egg, anchovies, olives, and sliced onions, moistened with olive oil.

Also noteworthy are the excellent thin-crusted pizzas (all flavours) and *pissaladière:* a savoury tart with a topping of onion, anchovies, black olives and sometimes tomatoes.

## Aperitifs and Wine

You can find the world's most sophisticated cocktails in the big hotel bars down here. If you order a martini, specify *un dry* or you might get Martini, the sweet Italian vermouth. Every little bar-café sells scotch, various imported and domestic beers, many non-alcoholic drinks. A very refreshing drink is *citron pressé* (fresh-squeezed lemon juice).

The number one local drink, of course, is *pastis*. This anise-flavoured yellow liquid turns milky when you add water—it's very refreshing on a warm day, provided you don't overdo it!

Vintage wines from all over France are available in the better restaurants, but for daily fare stick to the local product—white, red and especially rosé.

The best regional wines bear an *appellation contrôlée* (A.C.) label, guaranteeing place of origin and government-controlled quality. Four areas are given these labels: La Palette, Cassis, Bandol and Bellet.

La Palette (grown at Meyreuil, near Aix) comes from country thick with pines or herbs whose fragrances are said to permeate the wines. They exist in red and white (most notable—*Château Simone*). Cassis produces a fine red wine, but the flowery-light white wine is a special treat, particularly with shellfish.

Near Toulon, Bandol wine grows in a particularly favoured setting, producing some whites and lots of fruity rosés and reds, the latter particularly good; look for *Domaine des Tempiers*. Bellet is the fourth A.C. area, on precariously sloped vineyards above Nice, producing white, red and rosé wines. Further down the official scale, wines marked V.D.Q.S. *(vin délimité de qualité supérieure)* appear all over the south.

*Mid-morning snack in old Nice: socca, and outsized fried pancake.*

## Wine Guidelines

The fresh, slightly fruity qualities of Provençal white wine make it the perfect accompaniment to fish and shellfish. Sometimes the wines lack acidity because of the constant sunshine.

Rosé is much-maligned by wine snobs, who treat it as a poor compromise between white and red. But in Provence, it's another matter; even connoisseurs enjoy a well-chilled bottle with meals (particularly chicken or fish dishes) or as an aperitif. Rosés with the V.D.Q.S. label are reliably good; Tavel and Lirac, grown near Avignon, are famous. The colour of rosé is important: it should be light to rosy *pink,* not orange, which shows it has oxidized prematurely.

Red wines are gaining in both virtue and renown in the south. The A.C. areas now produce honourable reds, some to be drunk young and fresh (preferably cool), others age gracefully. *Château Vignelaure,* grown northeast of Aix, is more special.

Don't be surprised by the lack of vintage year on the labels of wine from Provence. Most are meant to be served very young (often within the year) and don't benefit from ageing.

## To Help You Order…

| | |
|---|---|
| Do you have a table? | **Avez-vous une table?** |
| Do you have a set-price menu? | **Avez-vous un menu?** |

| | |
|---|---|
| I'd like a/an/some… | **J'aimerais…** |

| | | | |
|---|---|---|---|
| beer | **une bière** | menu | **la carte** |
| butter | **du beurre** | milk | **du lait** |
| bread | **du pain** | mineral water | **de l'eau** |
| coffee | **un café** | | **minérale** |
| dessert | **un dessert** | potatoes | **des pommes** |
| egg | **un œuf** | | **de terre** |
| fish | **du poisson** | salad | **une salade** |
| fruit | **un fruit** | sandwich | **un sandwich** |
| glass | **un verre** | soup | **du potage** |
| ice-cream | **une glace** | sugar | **du sucre** |
| lemon | **du citron** | tea | **du thé** |
| meat | **de la viande** | wine | **du vin** |

## ...and Read the Menu

| | | | |
|---|---|---|---|
| **agneau** | lamb | **haricots verts** | string beans |
| **ail** | garlic | **jambon** | ham |
| **anchois** | anchovy | **langoustine** | prawn |
| **asperges** | asparagus | **langue** | tongue |
| **aubergine** | eggplant | **lapin** | rabbit |
| **bifteck** | steak | **lièvre** | hare |
| **bœuf** | beef | **loup de mer** | sea-bass |
| **caille** | quail | **macédoine de** | fruit salad |
| **calmar** | squid | **fruits** | |
| **canard/** | duck | **médaillon** | tenderloin |
| **caneton** | | **moules** | mussels |
| **cervelle** | brains | **moutarde** | mustard |
| **chèvre, cabri** | goat | **mulet** | grey mullet |
| **chou** | cabbage | **navets** | turnips |
| **chou-fleur** | cauliflower | **nouilles** | noodles |
| **choux de** | brussels sprouts | **oignons** | onions |
| **Bruxelles** | | **oseille** | sorrel |
| **concombre** | cucumber | **petits pois** | peas |
| **côte, côtelette** | chop, cutlet | **pintade** | guinea fowl |
| **courgettes** | baby marrow | **poisson** | fish |
| | (zucchini) | **poireaux** | leeks |
| **coquelet** | baby chicken | **pomme** | apples |
| **coquilles** | scallops | **porc** | pork |
| **Saint-Jacques** | | **poulet** | chicken |
| **crevettes** | shrimps | **prunes** | plums |
| **daurade** | gilt-head (fish) | **radis** | radishes |
| **écrevisse** | crayfish | **raisins** | grapes |
| **endive** | chicory (endive) | **ris de veau** | sweetbreads |
| **épinards** | spinach | **riz** | rice |
| **fenouil** | fennel | **rognons** | kidneys |
| **fèves** | broad beans | **rouget** | red mullet |
| **flageolets** | dried beans | **St. Pierre** | John Dory (fish) |
| **foie** | liver | **saucisse/** | sausage/dried |
| **fraises** | strawberries | **saucisson** | sausage |
| **framboises** | raspberries | **thon** | tunny (tuna) |
| **fruits de mer** | seafood | **truffes** | truffles |
| **gigot d'agneau** | leg of lamb | **veau** | veal |
| **glace** | ice, ice-cream | **volaille** | chicken |

99

# BLUEPRINT for a Perfect Trip

## How to Get There

The ever-changing air fares and airline regulations are complicated even for seasoned travellers. A reliable travel agent will be able to suggest a plan best suited to your timetable and budget.

When planning your trip, consult the Blueprint section in this book, especially for ENTRY AND CUSTOMS FORMALITIES and HOTELS AND ACCOMMODATION. If looked through in advance, this section can help you prepare for your visit to the French Riviera.

## BY AIR

### Scheduled flights

The main international airport serving the French Riviera is Nice-Côte d'Azur (see p. 105), which is linked frequently to many European and North African cities. However, most intercontinental flights use Paris as gateway city to France.

### Charter flights and package tours

**From the U.K. and Ireland:** Most tour organizers use scheduled airlines, although charter flights are available. Self-catering is popular, and there is a wide choice of accommodation available.

Most travel agents recommend cancellation insurance which prevents losing money in case illness or accident forces you to cancel your holiday.

**From North America:** Paris—Riviera package deals are frequently offered by tour organizers. Check the newspapers for the latest possibilities. There are charter flights available directly to the Riviera, or to many convenient gateway cities in Europe. Some companies also have "Discover France" bus vacations.

**From Australia and New Zealand:** There are no package tours to the French Riviera. Travel either by independent arrangement (the usual direct economy flight to Paris with unrestricted stopovers, or fly through another European gateway city with connections to Nice) or go on an air-and-car-hire arrangement.

## BY ROAD

From Paris you can follow the A-6/A-7/A-8 *autoroutes* (motorways/expressways). Via Lyons, Orange, Aix-en-Provence, you reach Fréjus (870 km./540 miles), Cannes (900 km./560 miles), Nice (940 km./585 miles). Motoring is also easy on the secondary roads in France which, though longer than the *autoroutes,* offer good scenery and are toll-free. From Paris, you can also put your car on a train *(train autos couchette* or *service autos express).*

## BY RAIL

Express trains operate from Paris to the Riviera (see also p. 120). Senior citizens can obtain a RES – *Rail Europ Senior Card* – which allows a reduction on all participating railways, including the French National Railways – S.N.C.F. Anyone under 26 years of age can purchase an *Inter-Rail Card* which allows one month's unlimited 2nd-class travel. People living outside Europe and North Africa can purchase a *Eurailpass* for unlimited rail travel in 16 European countries including France. This pass must be obtained before leaving home. The S.N.C.F.'s *France Vacances Special Ticket* is available to non-French residents for unlimited 1st and 2nd-class travel over the entire S.N.C.F. network.

# When to Go

July and August are the peak summer months when the crowds are drawn to France's sunniest beaches. These are the months when the climate is at its best, though spring and fall offer many days of mild weather with fewer visitors.

You may want to plan your holiday around one of the many events on the Riviera, such as Cannes' annual film festival in May.

Following are some monthly average temperatures:

|  |  | J | F | M | A | M | J | J | A | S | O | N | D |
|---|---|---|---|---|---|---|---|---|---|---|---|---|---|
| **Air temperature** | C | 9 | 9 | 11 | 13 | 17 | 20 | 23 | 22 | 20 | 17 | 12 | 9 |
|  | F | 48 | 48 | 52 | 55 | 63 | 68 | 73 | 72 | 68 | 63 | 54 | 48 |
| **Sea temperature** | C | 13 | 13 | 13 | 15 | 17 | 21 | 24 | 25 | 23 | 20 | 17 | 14 |
|  | F | 55 | 55 | 55 | 59 | 63 | 70 | 75 | 77 | 73 | 68 | 63 | 57 |

# France: Facts and Figures

**Geography:** Area 547,000 square kilometres (213,000 square miles). As the largest country in Western Europe, France shares frontiers with Belgium, Luxembourg, West Germany, Switzerland, Italy and Spain. Its highest point is Mont Blanc, Western Europe's tallest peak, at 4,800 metres (15,800 feet) above sea level. Four major rivers criss-cross the country: the Seine, the Loire, the Garonne and the Rhône; and Le Havre, Nantes, Bordeaux and Marseilles, France's four leading ports, lie at the mouths of these rivers.

**Population:** 57 million, of which about 4 ½ million are foreigners. 80% live in urban areas. Density: about 100 per square kilometre, or 255 per square mile.

**Major cities:** Paris (2.3 million, greater urban area 9 million), Marseilles (900,000), Lyons (450,000), Toulouse (350,000), Strasbourg (250,000).

**Government:** Republic, multi-party centralized democracy, headed by a president elected for seven years by universal suffrage. The Parliament consists of two houses, the National Assembly with 491 deputies and the Senate with 322 members. The country is divided into 95 *départements* (plus five overseas departments).

**Economy:** France is a major industrial country; the main industries are metal, machinery, shipbuilding, textiles, electrical and electronic equipment, clothing. Major exports: transport equipment, iron and steel products, textiles and clothing, agricultural products.

**Religion:** About 90% Catholic.

**Language:** French. Minorities speak Basque, Breton, Catalan, etc.

**French Riviera:** The Côte d'Azur forms an administrative region with Provence, and belongs within the Alpes-Maritimes and Var *départements*. The capital of Alpes-Maritimes (area: 4,300 square km./1,600 square miles) is Nice, with a population of about 360,000; the Var (area: 6,000 square km./2,300 square miles) has Toulon as its main city (about 185,000 inhabitants), France's main naval port in the Mediterranean.

# Planning Your Budget

The following are some prices in French francs (F). However, they must be regarded as approximate; inflation in France, as elsewhere, continues to rise steadily.

**Baby-sitters.** 25–30 F per hour, 80–120 F per day.

**Bicycle and moped rental.** Bicycle 120 F per day, moped 150 F, deposit minimum 1,000 F bicycle; 5,000 F moped.

**Boat rental.** Motor boat 600–900 F for four persons per day, sailing boat (medium) 2,000 F for four persons per weekend.

**Camping.** 120–220 F per night for four persons with tent or caravan (trailer).

**Car hire.** *Renault Super 5 GL* 379 F per day, 4.21 F per km., 2,250 F per week with unlimited mileage. *Renault 19* 449 F per day, 4.82 F per km., 2,007 F per week with unlimited mileage. *Renault 25 GTS* 634 F per day, 6.50 F per km., 4,500 F per week with unlimited mileage. Add 33.33% tax.

**Cigarettes.** French 7 F per packet of 20, foreign 10.30 F, cigars 3–70 F per piece.

**Entertainment.** Cinema 40 F, admission to discotheque 40–85 F, Casino admission 60–70 F, cabaret 100 F upwards (including meal).

**Guides.** 500 F for half day, 900 F per day, 125–150 F for each additional hour.

**Hairdressers.** *Woman's* haircut 100 F and up, blow-dry/shampoo and set 110 F and up, manicure 56 F and up. *Man's* haircut 70 F and up.

**Hotels** (per double room). ★★★★ 550–600 F, ★★★ 260–400 F, ★★ 210–320 F, ★ 100–140 F. Youth hostel 65–75 F.

**Meals and drinks.** Continental breakfast 25–40 F, tourist menu 60–95F, lunch/dinner in fairly good establishment 150–170 F, coffee 6 F, whisky or cocktail 25–35 F, beer/soft drink 15 F, cognac 25 F, bottle of wine 55 F and up.

**Museums.** 10 F.

**Sports.** Windsurf board about 60 F an hour, 600 F a week, instruction (with board, one lesson per day during one week) 400–500 F, water-skiing (6 minutes) 100 F, tennis 50 F an hour for a court, golf 70 F (9 hole), 200 F (18 hole) per day.

# An A–Z Summary of Practical Information and Facts

> A star (*) following an entry indicates that relevant prices are to be found on p.104.
>
> Listed after most entries is the appropriate French translation, usually in the singular, plus a number of phrases that may come in handy during your stay in France.

**AIRPORT** *(aéroport)*. The Nice-Côte d'Azur international airport (7 km. from Nice) is used by 35 airlines serving about 90 cities in 36 countries. Facilities include a currency-exchange bank, restaurants, bars, post office and car-rental agency as well as souvenir and duty-free shops. An airline bus leaves every 20 minutes for Nice, and another to Cannes stops at Antibes and Juan-les-Pins. A helicopter service connects the airport with Monaco.

The Marseilles-Provence airport has direct connections with French and major European cities, Corsica and North Africa.

Where's the bus for…? **D'où part le bus pour…?**

**BICYCLE and MOTORCYCLE RENTAL\*** *(location de bicyclettes/de motocyclettes)*. It's possible to hire bicycles, mopeds, called *vélomoteurs,* motorcycles and scooters in most towns of the French Riviera. Be prepared to lay out a deposit.

Minimum age to ride a moped is 14; for scooters from 50 to 125 cc., 16 years; over 125 cc. it's 18. Crash-helmets are obligatory. Enquire about rentals at your hotel or the local tourist office *(syndicat d'initiative)*.

**CAMPING\*** *(camping)*. Camping is extremely popular and very well organized in the South of France. There are over 300 officially recognized sites in the Alpes-Maritimes and the Var, most of them offering attractive locations and good facilities. These sites are classified from one to four stars depending on their amenities.

A *camping interdit* notice means the site is forbidden to campers, and the sign isn't a joke. You can always try to obtain an owner's permission to camp on private property in the region, but your chances are not very good.

**C**

Excellent booklets, such as *Camping–Côte d'Azur* (Menton to Cannes) can be obtained through the French Tourist Office in your country (see Tourist Information Offices). For the Var region, write to Promo-Var, rue Saunier, 83000 Toulon.

In the summer season, it's important to book in advance.

| | |
|---|---|
| May we camp here, please? | **Pouvons-nous camper ici, s'il vous plaît?** |

**CAR HIRE\*** *(location de voitures)*. All major car-hire firms in France handle French-made cars and occasionally foreign makes. Locally based firms generally charge less than the international companies but give little or no choice of where you can return the car.

To hire a car you must produce a valid driving licence (held for at least one year) and your passport. Some firms set a minimum age at 21, others 25. Holders of major credit cards are normally exempt from deposit payments, otherwise you must pay a substantial (refundable) deposit for a car. Third-party insurance is usually automatically included, and with an extra fee per day you can obtain full insurance coverage. Ask for any available seasonal deals.

| | |
|---|---|
| I'd like to hire a car tomorrow. | **Je voudrais louer une voiture demain.** |
| for one day/a week | **pour une journée/une semaine** |
| Please include full insurance. | **Avec assurance tous risques, s'il vous plaît.** |

**CIGARETTES, CIGARS, TOBACCO\*** *(cigarettes; cigares; tabac)*. Tobacco is a state monopoly in France, and the best place to buy your cigarettes is at an official *débit de tabac* (licensed tobacconist's). There are plenty of these – cafés and bars – bearing the conspicuous double red cone.

French cigarettes include brands with dark or light tobacco, with or without filter. Dozens of foreign brands are also available at higher prices. Pipe tobacco comes in a variety of cuts, from sweet to strong.

| | |
|---|---|
| A pack of…/A box of matches, please. | **Un paquet de…/Une boîte d'allumettes, s'il vous plaît.** |
| filter-tipped/without filter | **avec/sans filtre** |
| light/dark tobacco | **du tabac blond/brun** |

**CLOTHING** *(habillement)*. From May to October you can usually count on mild to hot weather and light summer clothing is best. On the other hand, be sure to take a warm jacket or wrap for cool evenings, and you'll appreciate a raincoat in the low season, even in late spring. Light wool clothing and an overcoat are necessary in the winter.

Anything goes on the Riviera, but each town has its code. Complete nudity is tolerated on some beaches (notably around Saint-Tropez and on the Ile du Levant); topless sunbathing is permitted in most places.

At night, *tenue correcte* is required in casinos—that is, a jacket and tie for men, dresses or neat slacks for women. When visiting churches, respectable clothing should be worn.

## COMMUNICATIONS

**Post Office** *(poste)*. You can identify French post offices by a sign with a stylized blue bird and/or the words *La Poste*. In cities the main post office is open from 8 a.m. to 5 p.m., Monday to Friday, and 8 a.m. to noon on Saturdays. In smaller towns the hours are from 8.30 a.m. to noon, and 2.30 to 5 or 6 p.m., Monday to Friday; 8 a.m. to noon on Saturdays.

In addition to normal mail service, you can make local or long-distance telephone calls, send telegrams and receive or send money at any time at the post office.

*Note:* You can also buy stamps at a tobacconist's.

**Mail** *(courrier)*. If you don't know ahead of time where you're staying, you can have your mail addressed to *poste restante* (general delivery) in any town. Towns with more than one post office keep mail at the main post office. Take your passport with you for identification.

**Telegrams** *(télégramme)*. All local post offices accept telegrams, domestic or overseas. You may also dictate a telegram over the telephone (dial 36.55).

**Telephone** *(téléphone)*. International or long-distance calls can be made from phone boxes, but if you need assistance in placing the call go to the post office or ask at your hotel. If you want to make a reverse-charge (collect) call, ask for *un appel en PCV* (pronounced: pay-say-vay). For a personal (person-to-person) call, specify *un appel avec préavis pour...* (naming the party you want to talk to). **107**

C  For long-distance calls within France, there are no area codes (just dial the 8-digit number of the person you want to call), *except* when telephoning from Paris or the Paris region to the provinces (dial 16 and wait for the dialling tone, then dial the 8-digit number of the subscriber) and from the provinces to Paris or the Paris region (dial 16, wait for the dialling tone, then dial 1 followed by the 8-digit number). If you need the assistance of an operator, dial 12.

To ring abroad from France, dial 19 followed, after the change of tone, by the country's number (listed in all boxes), the area code and the subscriber's number. If direct dialling is not available to that country or if you don't know the telephone number of the subscriber, dial 19 and wait for the tone, then dial 33.12 followed by the code number of the country in question to reach the operator (UK 44, U.S.A. and Canada 1). If you do not know the number of the country, call the international information, 12.

It's cheaper to make long-distance trunk calls after 9.30 p.m.

| | |
|---|---|
| express (special delivery) | **exprès** |
| airmail | **par avion** |
| registered | **recommandé** |

| | |
|---|---|
| A stamp for this letter/ postcard, please | **Un timbre pour cette lettre/ carte postale, s'il vous plaît.** |
| I want to send a telegram to… | **J'aimerais envoyer un télégramme à…** |
| Have you any mail for…? | **Avez-vous du courrier pour…?** |

## COMPLAINTS (*réclamation*)

**Hotels and restaurants.** Complaints should be referred to the owner or manager of the establishment in question. If you fail to obtain on-the-spot satisfaction for your complaint, you can refer the matter to the nearest police station (*commissariat de police*). If they cannot help, apply to the regional administration offices (*préfecture* or *sous-préfecture*), asking for the *service du tourisme*.

**Bad merchandise.** Complain at once to the proprietor or manager. In the event of gross abuse, register your complaint at the local *commissariat*.

| | |
|---|---|
| I'd like to make a complaint. | **J'ai une réclamation à faire.** |

## CONSULATES (*consulat*).
Most consulates are open, Monday to Friday, from 9 or 10 a.m. to 4 or 5 p.m. with an hour or so off for lunch. Schedules may change with the season, so it's best to call in advance.

**Australia:** (embassy) 4, rue Jean Rey, 75015 Paris; tel. 16 ~ (1) 40.59.33.00

**Canada:** 35, avenue Montaigne, 75008 Paris; tel. 16 ~ (1) 47.23.01.01

**Eire:** 152, boulevard John Fitzgerald Kennedy, Antibes; tel. 93.61.50.63

**United Kingdom:** 24, avenue du Prado, Marseilles 6e; tel. 91.53.43.32

**U.S.A.:** 12, boulevard Paul Peytral, Marseilles 6e; tel. 91.54.92.00; 36, rue Maréchal Joffre, 06000 Nice; tel. 93.88.89.55

**CONVERTER CHARTS.** For fluid and distance measures, see pages 111–112. France uses the metric system.

**Temperature**

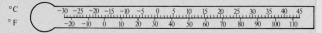

**Length**

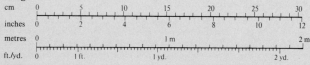

**Weight**

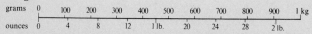

**COURTESIES.** See also MEETING PEOPLE. The sunny climate of southern France makes for a good-natured but impetuous temperament. Though you'll hear lots of shouting, it's usually high-spirited discussion rather than real argument, and the shopkeepers and restaurant personnel are far more relaxed than in Paris.

In restaurants and cafés, *garçon* is the customary way to call a waiter (*mademoiselle* for a waitress), or you can simply say *s'il vous plaît*. The *maître d'hôtel* (headwaiter) and *sommelier* (wine steward) are addressed as *monsieur*.

French people kiss or shake hands when greeting each other or saying goodbye. When you're introduced to someone or meeting a friend you're expected to shake hands at least. Close friends are kissed on both cheeks.

**C**    If you stop a policeman or passerby to ask for directions, start with *excusez-moi, Monsieur/Madame*. Use your French, no matter how faulty, unless the person you're speaking to seems impatient and speaks your language well. Your effort will be appreciated.

**CRIME and THEFT** (*délit; vol*). If you have items of real value, keep them in the hotel safe and obtain a receipt for them; it's a good idea to leave large amounts of money and even your passport there as well.

Another wise precaution is to keep any valuables out of sight especially when you leave your car. Any loss or theft should be reported at once to the nearest *commissariat de police* or *gendarmerie* (see POLICE).

**D**    **DRIVING IN FRANCE.** To take a car into France, you will need:

- A valid driving licence
- Car registration papers
- A red warning triangle and a set of spare bulbs

The green insurance card is no longer obligatory, but full insurance coverage is strongly recommended. Drivers and front-seat passengers are required by law to wear seat belts. Children under 10 may not travel in the front (unless the car has no back seat). Driving on a provisional licence is not permitted in France. Minimum age is 18.

**Driving conditions:** The rules are the same as elsewhere on the Continent – drive on the right, overtake on the left, yield right of way to all vehicles coming from the right (except on roundabouts/traffic circles), unless otherwise indicated.

**Speed limits:** On dry roads, 130 kph on toll motorways (expressways), 110 kph on dual carriageways (divided highways), 90 kph on all other roads, and 45 to 50 kph in built-up areas. When roads are wet, all limits are reduced by 10 kph. The word *rappel* means a restriction is continued. Fines for exceeding the speed limits are payable on the spot.

The French style of driving can be terrifying if you're not used to it, with plenty of speed and daring overtaking. Stick to your own pace and keep a safe distance between yourself and the vehicle in front.

**Road conditions:** French roads are designated by an A, standing for *autoroute* (motorway); an N for national highways; a D for *départementale*, or regional roads; or a V for local roads (*chemins vicinaux*). In recent years, road surfaces have been greatly improved. The *nationales,* or major highways, are good on the whole but often not as wide as they could be, especially at the time when most French people go on holiday: the 1st and 15th of July, the 1st and 15th of August and the 1st of September.

The motorways are excellent and owned by public companies which usually charge tolls according to vehicle size and distance travelled. All amenities (restaurants, toilets, service stations, etc.) are available, plus orange S.O.S. telephones every 2 kilometres.

Many tourists like to travel on secondary roads at a more leisurely pace with better views. Sometimes you'll find alternative routes *(itinéraires bis)* sign-posted along the way by emerald-green arrows.

**Parking:** In town centres, most street parking is metered. In blue zones (parking spaces marked with a blue line) you must display a *disque de stationnement* or parking clock (obtainable from petrol stations or stationers), which you set to show when you arrived and when you must leave. Some streets have alternate parking on either side of the street according to which half of the month it is (the dates are marked on the signs).

**Breakdowns:** Towing and on-the-spot repairs can be made by local garages, and spare parts are readily available for European cars. It's wise to take out some form of internationally valid breakdown insurance before leaving home, and always ask for an estimate *before* undertaking repairs.

**Traffic police:** The *gendarmerie* patrols the roads and motorways in cars or on powerful motorcycles. Always in pairs, they are courteous and helpful but extremely severe on lawbreakers and have authority to fine offenders on the spot.

**Fuel and oil:** Fuel *(essence)* is available in super (98 octane), normal (90 octane), lead-free *(sans plomb,* 95 octane) and diesel *(gas-oil).* All grades of motor oil are on sale. It's usual to tip service-station attendants for any additional services rendered.

**Fluid measures**

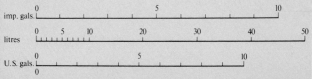

## D Distance

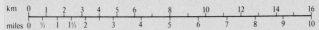

**Road signs:** Most road signs are the standard pictographs used throughout Europe, but you may encounter these written signs as well:

| | |
|---|---|
| **Accotements non stabilisés** | Soft shoulders |
| **Chaussée déformée** | Bad road surface |
| **Déviation** | Diversion (detour) |
| **Douane** | Customs |
| **Péage** | Toll |
| **Priorité à droite** | Yield to traffic from right |
| **Ralentir** | Slow |
| **Sauf riverains** | Entry prohibited except for inhabitants of street |
| **Serrez à droite/gauche** | Keep right/left |
| **Stationnement interdit** | No parking |

| | |
|---|---|
| (international) driving licence | **permis de conduire (international)** |
| car registration papers | **carte grise** |

| | |
|---|---|
| Are we on the right road for…? | **Sommes-nous sur la route de…?** |

| | |
|---|---|
| Fill the tank, please | **Le plein, s'il vous plaît.** |
| lead-free/normal/super | **sans plomb/normale/super** |

| | |
|---|---|
| Check the oil/tires/battery. | **Veuillez contrôler l'huile/ les pneus/la batterie** |

| | |
|---|---|
| I've had a breakdown. | **Ma voiture est en panne.** |
| There's been an accident. | **Il y a eu un accident.** |

**DRUGS.** The possession, use and distribution of drugs are criminal offences. Prison sentences for offenders can be extremely severe, and suspects may have to wait a considerable time for trial – in jail.

## E ELECTRIC CURRENT.

220-volt, 50-cycle A.C. is now universal. British and American visitors using electric appliances should remember to buy a Continental adaptor plug before leaving home. They can also be bought in some electric supply shops *(magasins d'électricité)* or *drogueries*.

| | |
|---|---|
| **112** an adaptor plug/a battery | **une prise de raccordement/une pile** |

**EMERGENCIES** *(urgence).* For real emergencies you can get assistance
anywhere in France by dialling the number 17 for the police *(Police-Secours);* call number 18 for the fire brigade *(pompiers)* which also comes
for such emergencies as drowning. For less pressing problems, see
separate entries in this section such as CONSULATES, MEDICAL CARE,
POLICE, etc.

Though we hope you'll never need them, here are a few key words you
might like to learn in advance:

| Careful! | **Attention!** | Help! | **Au secours!** |
| Fire! | **Au feu!** | Police! | **Police!** |

**ENTRY FORMALITIES and CUSTOMS** *(douane).* Nationals of EEC
countries need only a valid passport to enter France. A British Visitor's
Passport is also accepted. Nationals of other countries should check with
the French consulate to see if they need a visa. Though European and
North American residents are not subject to any health requirements, visitors from further afield may require a smallpox vaccination. Check with
your travel agent before departure.

The following chart shows what main items you may take into France:

| Into: | Cigarettes | | Cigars | | Tobacco | Spirits | | Wine |
|-------|-----------|-----|--------|-----|---------|---------|-----|------|
| France 1) | 200 | or | 50 | or | 250 g. | 1 l. | and | 2 l. |
| 2) | 300 | or | 75 | or | 400 g. | 1½ l. | and | 5 l. |
| 3) | 400 | or | 100 | or | 500 g. | 1 l. | and | 2 l. |
| Canada | 200 | and | 50 | and | 900 g. | 1.1 l. | or | 1 l. |
| Eire 1) | 200 | or | 50 | or | 250 g. | 1 l. | and | 2 l. |
| 2) | 300 | or | 75 | or | 400 g. | 1½ l. | and | 5 l. |
| U.K. 1) | 200 | or | 50 | or | 250 g. | 1 l. | and | 2 l. |
| 2) | 300 | or | 75 | or | 400 g. | 1 ½ l. | and | 2 l. |
| U.S.A. | 200 | and | 100 | and | 4) | 1 l. | or | 1 l. |

1) If arriving from EEC countries with duty-free items or from other European
   countries.
2) If arriving from EEC countries with non-duty free items.
3) Residents outside Europe.
4) A reasonable quantity.

**Currency restrictions:** There's no limit on the importation or exportation
of French francs or foreign currencies or traveller's cheques.

113

**F**  **FOREST FIRES.** Every summer, alas, they occur, more or less serious, more or less destructive. Do your part in preventing them: put out cigarettes carefully, do not light fires, and be especially careful if using a grill or primus stove on a picnic. Only a spark does it, and they catch on in no time.

**G**  **GUIDES and INTERPRETERS*** *(guide; interprète).* Local *syndicats d'initiative* (see TOURIST INFORMATION OFFICES) can supply or direct you to qualified official guides and interpreters if you want a personally conducted tour or any linguistic assistance. Guides engaged for a whole day should be offered lunch.

Bus companies from Nice and Cannes also offer many guided tours. It's customary to tip the guide.

| | |
|---|---|
| We'd like an English-speaking guide. | **Nous aimerions un guide parlant anglais.** |
| I need an English interpreter. | **J'ai besoin d'un interprète anglais.** |

**H**  **HAIRDRESSERS*** and **BARBERS** *(coiffeur).* Prices vary widely according to the class of establishment, but rates are often displayed in the window.

**Tipping:** Most establishments include *service* in the price, but it's customary to give a little something to the person who washes your hair, and a small tip to the stylist.

| | |
|---|---|
| haircut | **coupe** |
| simple cut | **coupe simple** |
| shampoo and set | **shampooing et mise en plis** |
| blow-dry | **un brushing** |
| a colour chart | **un nuancier** |
| a colour rinse/hair-dye | **un rinçage/une coloration** |
| Not too much off (here). | **Pas trop court (ici).** |
| A little more off (here). | **Un peu plus court (ici).** |

**HOTELS and ACCOMMODATION*** *(hôtel; logement).* See also CAMPING and YOUTH HOSTELS. France offers a huge variety of hotel accommodation to suit every taste and pocket.

Tourist offices and *syndicats d'initiative* can supply local hotel lists. **H**
Note that a hotel labelled simply *Hôtel* may not have a restaurant, especially in big towns. The *Accueil de France* offices located in tourist offices in the cities will make room reservations for a small fee. Major airports and railway stations have hotel reservation desks.

*Note: Hôtel de Ville* is not a hotel, but the town hall.

**Other accommodation:** This can run from the relatively modest *gîte* and *logis de France* to luxurious settings like the *château-hôtel* and *relais de campagne,* where prices can be very high.

**House rental:** Tourist offices can recommend agencies with complete lists of available houses and apartments to let. In full season, you should book well ahead.

| | |
|---|---|
| a double/single room | **une chambre double/simple** |
| with/without bath | **avec/sans bains** |
| What's the rate per night? | **Quel est le prix pour une nuit?** |
| Must I take meals? | **Est-ce que la pension est obligatoire?** |
| I'm looking for a flat to rent for a month. | **Je cherche un appartement à louer pour un mois.** |

**LANGUAGE.** Real southerners have a charming, droll accent, drawing **L**
out their syllables in a way you don't hear elsewhere. The usual nasal French "en" ending becomes a hard "ng" *(chien* sounds like *chieng).*

In addition, you'll hear all sorts of rolling, vaguely Italianate dialects, especially Niçois and Monegasque. See also the box on page 14.

The Berlitz phrase book FRENCH FOR TRAVELLERS covers almost all situations you're likely to encounter in your travels in France. In addition, the Berlitz French-English/English-French pocket dictionary contains a 12,500 word glossary of each language, plus a menu-reader supplement.

| | |
|---|---|
| Good morning/Good afternoon | **Bonjour** |
| Good afternoon/Good evening | **Bonsoir** |
| Please | **S'il vous plaît** |
| Thank you | **Merci** |
| You're welcome | **Je vous en prie** |
| Goodbye | **Au revoir** |

**115**

**L**  **LAUNDRY and DRY-CLEANING** *(blanchisserie; teinturerie; nettoyage à sec).* You'll still see some women in the Midi beating their laundry against the stone in the public fountain *lavoirs.* But modern facilities are growing fast.

If your hotel will not take care of laundry or cleaning, you can have clothes cleaned quickly and cheaply in chain dry-cleaners (not recommended, however, for fragile fabrics or difficult spots). Better care takes longer and is more expensive; prices vary according to fabric and cut.

**LOST PROPERTY** *(objets trouvés);* **LOST CHILDREN.** Check first at your hotel desk and if you have no success there report the loss to the nearest *commissariat de police* or *gendarmerie* (see POLICE).

Restaurant and café personnel are quite honest about keeping objects forgotten or lost until the owner reclaims them, or in the case of wallets, turning them over to the police.

If you lose a child, you'll find people very helpful. It should be reported to any policeman *(agent de police)* on duty or the nearest *commissariat* or *gendarmerie.* In any case, don't let young children out of your sight in crowded places.

| | |
|---|---|
| I've lost my child/wallet/ handbag/passport. | **J'ai perdu mon enfant/portefeuille/ sac/passeport.** |

**M**  **MAPS** *(carte; plan).* Various detailed topographical and road maps exist for motorists and hikers. Particularly useful is Michelin's No. 84, and the detailed map of the Alpes-Maritimes, No. 195. Falk-Verlag, who provided the maps for this guide, publishes a map of France.

| | |
|---|---|
| Do you have a map of the city/of the region? | **Avez-vous un plan de la ville/ une carte de la région?** |

**MEDICAL CARE.** See also EMERGENCIES. To be at ease, make sure your health insurance policy covers any illness or accident while on holiday. If not, ask your insurance representative, automobile association or travel agent for details of special travel insurance.

You'll find well-trained doctors and specialists in the south of France. If you're taken ill or have a toothache, consult your hotel receptionist, who can probably recommend an English-speaking doctor or dentist. In Cannes, the Sunnybank Anglo-American Hospital is staffed by British nurses:

**116**  133, avenue du Petit-Juas; tel. 93.68.29.96

Visitors from EEC countries with corresponding health insurance facilities are entitled to medical and hospital treatment under the French social security system. Before leaving home, make sure you find out about the appropriate form(s) required to obtain this benefit in case of need. Doctors who belong to the French social security system *(médecins conventionnés)* charge the minimum.

Chemists' *(pharmacie)* with green crosses are helpful in dealing with minor ailments or in finding a nurse *(infirmière)* if you need injections or other special care.

**Health** *(santé)*. The "tourist's complaint" that hits many travellers is not due to drinking tap water, which is safe in towns all over France. Fatigue, too much sun, change of diet and over-indulgence are the main causes of most minor complaints. Be careful about over-eating and, especially, drinking. French mineral water is a good thirst quencher and helps to digest meals. Serious gastro-intestinal problems lasting more than a day or two should be looked after by a doctor.

| | |
|---|---|
| Where's the chemist on duty? | **Où est la pharmacie de garde?** |
| I need a doctor. | **Il me faut un médecin.** |
| a dentist | **un dentiste** |
| an upset stomach | **mal à l'estomac** |
| a fever | **de la fièvre** |
| sunburn | **un coup de soleil** |
| I've a pain here. | **J'ai mal ici.** |

**MEETING PEOPLE.** See also COURTESIES. The French Riviera has been for many years a very cosmopolitan and popular resort area, not only for foreigners but for the northern French themselves. Something of a blasé attitude towards tourists may be met with in the overfrequented spots, while off the beaten track spontaneous warmth and kindness are as alive as ever.

**Minitel:** The Minitel has invaded most French homes and public buildings. It's used for everything from looking up phone numbers to booking theatre tickets to ordering a case of Bordeaux. A little brochure – "Passeport Tourisme Minitel" – with operating instructions in English and a list of useful codes is available from tourist offices. Some of the 7,000 services are in English.

# M | MONEY MATTERS

**Currency** *(monnaie)*. For currency restrictions, see ENTRY FORMALITIES and CUSTOMS. The *franc*, France's monetary unit (abbreviated F or FF) is divided into 100 *centimes*. Current coins include 5-, 10-, 20- and 50-centime pieces as well as 1-, 2-, 5- and 10-franc pieces. Banknotes come in denominations of 20, 50, 100, 200 and 500 francs.

Many French people still like to express prices in "old" francs *(anciens francs)* – although the system changed in the 1950s; 100 of them equal 1 "new" franc. In shops, however, only new francs are referred to.

**Banks and Currency-Exchange Offices** *(banques; bureau de change)*. Hours may vary, but most banks are open Monday to Friday from 9 to 11.30 a.m. and 1.30 to 5 p.m. Some currency-exchange offices operate on Saturdays as well. At Monte Carlo, a *bureau de change* opposite the Casino is open every day.

Your hotel will usually change currency or traveller's cheques into francs, but the rate is not favourable – nor is it in shops and casinos where traveller's cheques are often accepted. Always take your passport along when you go to change money.

**Credit Cards** *(carte de crédit)*. Most hotels, smarter restaurants, some boutiques, car-hire firms and tourist-related businesses in towns accept certain credit cards.

**Traveller's cheques** *(chèque de voyage)*. Hotels, travel agents and many shops accept them, although the exchange rate is invariably better at a bank. Don't forget to take your passport when going to cash a traveller's cheque. Eurocheques are also accepted.

**Prices** *(prix)*. The cost of living on the Riviera is generally high, but it is possible to have a good time on a budget if you choose carefully. (The further you get away from the coast, the more likely you are to find reasonably priced hotels and restaurants.)

Official prices are always posted prominently in public establishments, including cafés, bars, hotels and restaurants.

| | |
|---|---|
| Could you give me some (small) change? | **Pouvez-vous me donner de la (petite) monnaie?** |
| I want to change some pounds/dollars. | **Je voudrais changer des livres sterling/des dollars.** |
| Do you accept traveller's cheques? | **Acceptez-vous les chèques de voyage?** |
| Can I pay with this credit card? | **Puis-je payer avec cette carte de crédit?** |

**NEWSPAPERS and MAGAZINES** *(journal; revue)*. In addition to French national and local papers, most towns also have British newspapers for sale. The Paris edition of the *International Herald Tribune* is available at main newsagents in cities and large towns.

Magazines in many languages are available at larger news-stands.

| | |
|---|---|
| Have you any English-language newspapers? | **Avez-vous des journaux en anglais?** |

**PETS** *(animal domestique)*. If you want to bring your pet dog or cat along, you'll need a health and rabies inoculation certificate for the animal to enter the country. Many hotels and restaurants allow pets, but check first.

**PHOTOGRAPHY** *(photographie)*. The coast is a photographer's dream, with plenty of light, varied scenery and colours of every intensity from soft pastel shades to the most vibrant hues. Certain museums will give you permission to photograph inside.

All popular film makes and sizes are available in France. Rapid development is possible, but quite expensive.

| | |
|---|---|
| I'd like a film for this camera. | **J'aimerais un film pour cet appareil.** |
| a black-and-white film | **un film noir et blanc** |
| a film for colour prints | **un film couleurs** |
| a colour-slide film | **un film de diapositives** |
| How long will it take to develop this film? | **Combien de temps faut-il pour développer ce film?** |
| Can I take a picture of you? | **Puis-je vous prendre en photo?** |

**POLICE** *(police)*. In cities and larger towns you'll see the blue uniformed *police municipale;* they are the local police force who keep order, investigate crime and direct traffic. Outside of the main towns are the *gendarmes*—they wear blue trousers and black jackets with white belts and are also responsible for traffic and crime investigation.

The C.R.S. police *(Compagnies Républicaines de Sécurité)* are a national security force responsible to the Ministry of the Interior and are called in for emergencies and special occasions. The *gendarmerie* patrol the roads.

In case of need, dial 17 anywhere in France for police help.

| | |
|---|---|
| Where's the nearest police station? | **Où est le poste de police le plus proche?** |

**PUBLIC HOLIDAYS** *(jours fériés)*

| | | |
|---|---|---|
| January 1 | *Jour de l'An* | New Year's Day |
| May 1 | *Fête du Travail* | Labour Day |
| May 8 | *Fête de la Libération* | Victory Day (1945) |
| July 14 | *Fête Nationale* | Bastille Day |
| August 15 | *Assomption* | Assumption |
| November 1 | *Toussaint* | All Saints' Day |
| November 11 | *Anniversaire de l'Armistice* | Armistice Day |
| December 25 | *Noël* | Christmas Day |
| Movable dates: | *Lundi de Pâques* | Easter Monday |
| | *Ascension* | Ascension |
| | *Lundi de Pentecôte* | Whit Monday |

These are the national French holidays. See page 81 for details of local celebrations and events.

## PUBLIC TRANSPORT

**Buses** *(autobus, autocar)*. Larger towns and cities like Cannes, Nice, Toulon and Monte Carlo have urban bus services – a particularly good way to get around. Inter-city bus services all along the coast and into the hinterland are efficient, comfortable, inexpensive and fairly frequent.

**Taxis** *(taxi)*. Taxis are clearly marked and available in all the larger towns. If the cab is unmetered, or you have a fair distance to go, ask the fare beforehand.

**Trains** *(train)*. The French National Railways (S.N.C.F.) operate a widespread network. Services are fast, punctual and comfortable. In season, at least ten trains a day (car train and TGV – *train à grande vitesse*) run from Paris' Gare de Lyon to Nice, and there is also a daily sleeper which carries cars. A major line links Marseilles and Menton along the Mediterranean coast. An old-fashioned steam train on the Nice-Digne line makes pleasant tours of the Provence countryside in season.

Trains are also a good way of getting around the coast quickly and cheaply in the height of summer traffic. The train ride from Menton to Nice, for example, lasts half an hour; by car or bus the same trip may take you an hour or more.

S.N.C.F. offer various categories of ticket, like Billet Touristique, Billet de Groupes, Billet de Famille, France-Vacances, etc. Inquire at the nearest tourist office or railway information counter. Eurailpasses and Inter-rail cards are valid in France.

| | |
|---|---|
| When's the next bus/train to…? | **Quand part le prochain bus/ train pour…?** |
| When's the best train to…? | **A quelle heure part le meilleur train pour…?** |
| single (one-way) | **aller simple** |
| return (round-trip) | **aller et retour** |
| first/second class | **première/deuxième classe** |
| I'd like to make seat reservations. | **J'aimerais réserver des places.** |

**RADIO and TV** *(radio; télévision)*. There are four main TV channels in France. Some hotels have television lounges; a few have TV in the rooms. All programmes (except for a few late films) are in French. Monte Carlo television can also be picked up in most places along the coast.

You can easily tune in to BBC programmes on either short- or medium-wave radios. In summer the French radio broadcasts news and information in English. Local newspapers have the details. Radio 104 FM transmits in English all day.

**RELIGIOUS SERVICES.** France is a predominantly Roman Catholic country. Ask your hotel receptionist or the local tourist office for information about the location and times of services in English. There are English-speaking Protestant churches and synagogues in Cannes, Menton, Monaco, Nice and Saint-Raphaël. Non-Catholic services are called *cultes*.

| | |
|---|---|
| Where is the Protestant church/ synagogue? | **Où se trouve le temple protestant/ la synagogue?** |

**TIME DIFFERENCES.** France follows Greenwich Mean Time + 1, and in spring the clocks are put forward one hour. If your country does the same, the time difference remains constant for most of the year.

| Los Angeles | Chicago | New York | London | **Nice** |
|---|---|---|---|---|
| 3 a.m. | 5 a.m. | 6 a.m. | 11 a.m. | **noon** |

| | | |
|---|---|---|
| What time is it? | **Quelle heure est-il?** | **121** |

**T** **TIPPING.** A 10 to 15% service charge is generally included automatically in hotel and restaurant bills. Rounding off the overall bill helps round off friendships with waiters, too. It is also in order to hand the bellboys, doormen, filling station attendants, etc., a coin or two for their service.

The chart below gives some suggestions as to what to leave.

| | |
|---|---|
| Hotel porter, per bag | 5 F |
| Hotel maid, per week | 20–50 F |
| Lavatory attendant | 1 F |
| Waiter | 5–10 % (optional) |
| Taxi driver | 10–15 % |
| Hairdresser/Barber | 10 % |
| Tour guide, half day | 10–20 F |

**TOILETS** *(toilettes).* Clean public conveniences are still not all that common in France, and the stand-up toilet facilities can be rather harrowing. If there is no light-switch, the light will usually go on when you lock the door. Three-star W.C.'s do exist, mostly in better hotels and restaurants.

Café facilities are generally free, but you should order at least a coffee if you use the toilet. A saucer with small change on it means that a tip is expected. The women's toilets may be marked *Dames;* the men's either *Messieurs* or *Hommes.*

Where are the toilets, please?    **Où sont les toilettes, s'il vous plaît?**

**TOURIST INFORMATION OFFICES** *(office du tourisme).* French national tourist offices can help you plan your holiday and will supply you with a wide range of colourful, informative brochures and maps.

Some addresses:

**Canada:** 1981, McGill College Avenue, Esso Tower, Suite 490, Montreal, Que. H3A 2W9; tel.: (514) 288-4264

1 Dundas St. W, Suite 2405, P.O. Box 8, Toronto, Ont. M5G 1Z3; tel.: (416) 593-4717

**United Kingdom:** 178, Piccadilly, London W1V 0AL; tel. (071) 493-6594

**U.S.A.** 645 N. Michigan Ave., Suite 430, Chicago IL 60611; tel.: (312) 337-6301

9401 Wilshire Blvd., Room 840, Beverly Hills CA 90212; tel.: (213) 272-2661

610 5th Ave., New York NY 10020; tel.: (212) 757-1125

1 Hallidie Plaza, San Francisco, CA 94102; tel.: (415) 986-4174

On the spot:

| | |
|---|---|
| **Cannes:** | Office du Tourisme, Palais des Festivals, La Croisette; tel. 93.39.24.53 |
| **Marseilles:** | Office Municipal du Tourisme, 4, La Canebière; tel. 91.54.91.11 |
| **Monaco:** | Direction du Tourisme et des Congrès, 2a, boulevard des Moulins; tel. 93.30.87.01 |
| **Nice:** | Office du Tourisme, 1, Esplanade John Fitzgerald Kennedy; tel. 93.92.82.82 and at the airport (parking Ferber) Syndicat d'Initiative, central railway station |

Local tourist information offices *(syndicat d'initiative)* are invaluable sources of information (from maps to hotel lists and other miscellaneous items) in all French towns. They are usually found near the town's centre and often have a branch at the railway station. Opening hours vary, but the general rule is 8.30 or 9 a.m. to noon and from 2 to 6 or 7 p.m., every day except Sunday.

Where's the tourist office, please? **Où est le syndicat d'initiative,
s'il vous plaît?**

**WATER** *(eau)*. Tap water is safe throughout the country, except when marked *eau non potable* (not safe for drinking). A wide variety of mineral

water can be found on sale everywhere.

a bottle of mineral water **une bouteille d'eau minérale**
fizzy/still **gazeuse/non gazeuse**

Is this drinking water? **Est-ce de l'eau potable?**

**YOUTH HOSTELS** *(auberge de jeunesse)*. Your national youth hostel association can give you all the details, or contact the Fédération Unie des

Auberges de Jeunesse, 6, rue Mesnil, 75116 Paris; tel. 16~(1) 45.05.13.14.

## DAYS OF THE WEEK

| Sunday | **dimanche** | Thursday | **jeudi** |
| Monday | **lundi** | Friday | **vendredi** |
| Tuesday | **mardi** | Saturday | **samedi** |
| Wednesday | **mercredi** | | |

## MONTHS

| January | **janvier** | July | **juillet** |
| February | **février** | August | **août** |
| March | **mars** | September | **septembre** |
| April | **avril** | October | **octobre** |
| May | **mai** | November | **novembre** |
| June | **juin** | December | **décembre** |

## NUMBERS

| 0 | **zéro** | 19 | **dix-neuf** |
| 1 | **un, une** | 20 | **vingt** |
| 2 | **deux** | 21 | **vingt et un** |
| 3 | **trois** | 22 | **vingt-deux** |
| 4 | **quatre** | 23 | **vingt-trois** |
| 5 | **cinq** | 30 | **trente** |
| 6 | **six** | 40 | **quarante** |
| 7 | **sept** | 50 | **cinquante** |
| 8 | **huit** | 60 | **soixante** |
| 9 | **neuf** | 70 | **soixante-dix** |
| 10 | **dix** | 71 | **soixante et onze** |
| 11 | **onze** | 80 | **quatre-vingts** |
| 12 | **douze** | 90 | **quatre-vingt-dix** |
| 13 | **treize** | 100 | **cent** |
| 14 | **quatorze** | 101 | **cent un** |
| 15 | **quinze** | 126 | **cent vingt-six** |
| 16 | **seize** | 200 | **deux cents** |
| 17 | **dix-sept** | 300 | **trois cents** |
| 18 | **dix-huit** | 1000 | **mille** |

## SOME USEFUL EXPRESSIONS

| | |
|---|---|
| yes/no | **oui/non** |
| please/thank you | **s'il vous plaît/merci** |
| excuse me | **excusez-moi** |
| you're welcome | **je vous en prie** |
| where/when/how | **où/quand/comment** |
| how long/how far | **combien de temps/à quelle distance** |
| yesterday/today/tomorrow | **hier/aujourd'hui/demain** |
| day/week/month/year | **jour/semaine/mois/année** |
| left/right | **gauche/droite** |
| up/down | **en haut/en bas** |
| good/bad | **bon/mauvais** |
| big/small | **grand/petit** |
| cheap/expensive | **bon marché/cher** |
| hot/cold | **chaud/froid** |
| old/new | **vieux/neuf** |
| open/closed | **ouvert/fermé** |
| here/there | **ici/là** |
| free (vacant)/occupied | **libre/occupé** |
| early/late | **tôt/tard** |
| easy/difficult | **facile/difficile** |
| Does anyone here speak English? | **Y a-t-il quelqu'un ici qui parle anglais?** |
| What does this mean? | **Que signifie ceci?** |
| I don't understand. | **Je ne comprends pas.** |
| Please write it down. | **Ecrivez-le-moi, s'il vous plaît.** |
| Is there an admission charge? | **Faut-il payer pour entrer?** |
| Waiter/Waitress! | **S'il vous plaît!** |
| I'd like… | **J'aimerais…** |
| How much is that? | **C'est combien?** |
| Have you something less expensive? | **Avez-vous quelque chose de moins cher?** |
| What time is it? | **Quelle heure est-il?** |
| Help me please. | **Aidez-moi, s'il vous plaît.** |

# Index

An asterisk (*) next to a page number indicates a map reference. For sites and town names starting with an article (le, la, les, l') see the basic word. For index to Practical Information, see inside front cover.

149/204 MUD